I0709744

# VINCENT VAN GOGH

## Advice for the Soul

The Van Gogh Museum is grateful that you are
directly contributing to the preservation of
Van Gogh's legacy and art collection so that
it may continue to inspire and be shared with
future generations.

vangoghmuseum.nl

Digital edition: Vincent van Gogh, The Letters.
Ed. Leo Jansen, Hans Luijten and Nienke Bakker.
Van Gogh Museum & Huygens Institute,
Amsterdam 2009.

vangoghletters.org



First published in 2024 by September Publishing



Text design by Studio April

Printed in Poland on paper from responsibly
managed, sustainable sources by Hussar Books

ISBN 9781914613685

10 9 8 7 6 5 4 3 2 1

September Publishing
an imprint of Duckworth Books Ltd
septemberpublishing.org

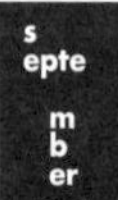

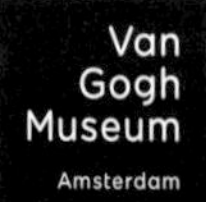

# CONTENTS

In 1888, Vincent van Gogh wrote to Paul Gauguin, a fellow artist, to invite him to help set up a studio that would act as a creative refuge for others. While Van Gogh's commitment to his own path sometimes brought him into conflict with those close to him, he believed passionately in the essential goodness of humankind, and in many of his artworks he seeks to capture the sparks of divinity that he finds in the living world. Vincent was the eldest of six and it's perhaps not surprising that he freely shares advice and insights in his letters, touching on subjects such as purpose, hope and love. The quotes in this volume come from his extensive correspondence, which has been translated from Dutch and French by

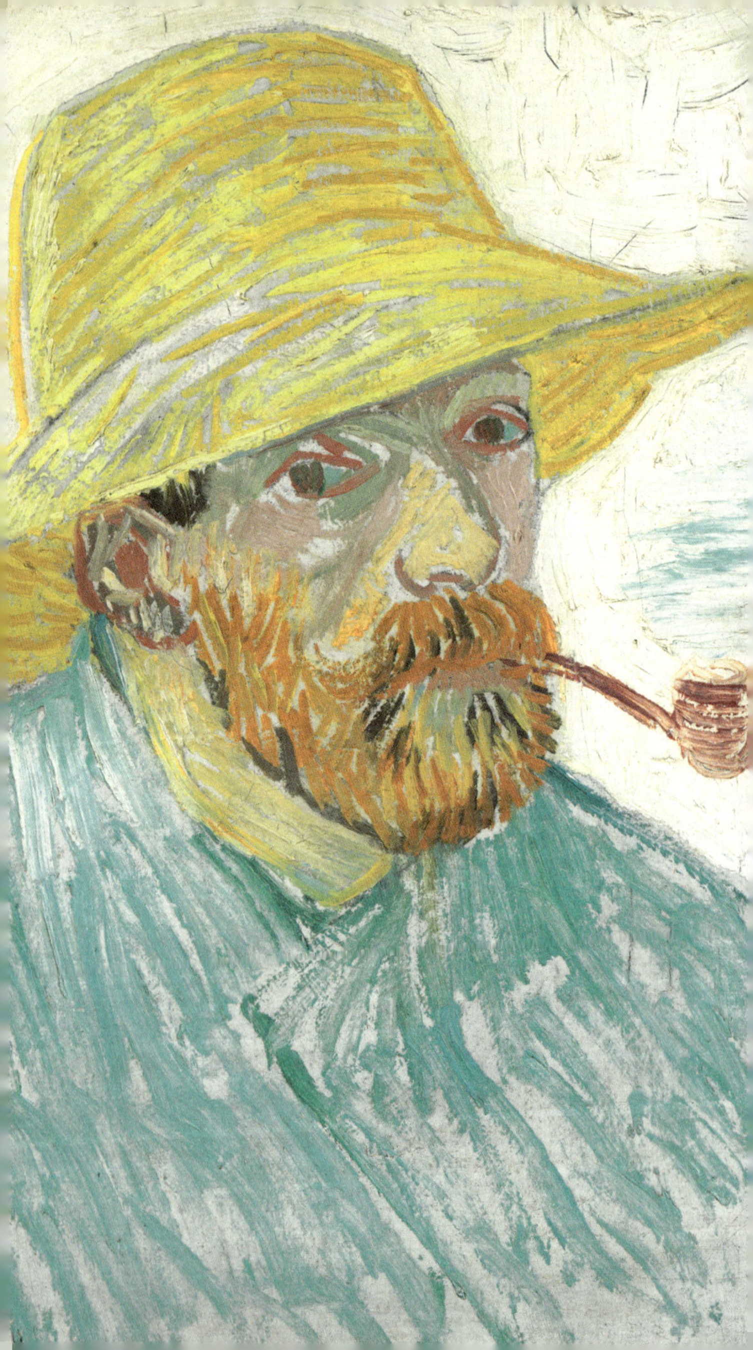

the Van Gogh Letters Project, a product
of fifteen years of research at the
Van Gogh Museum and the Huygens
Institute. The accompanying images by
Vincent are from the Van Gogh Museum's
collection. With their celebration of
humanity, his letters, sketches and
paintings show the way towards a
greater sense of belonging, harmony
and fulfilment of the soul.

*Sue Belfrage*

# COURAGE

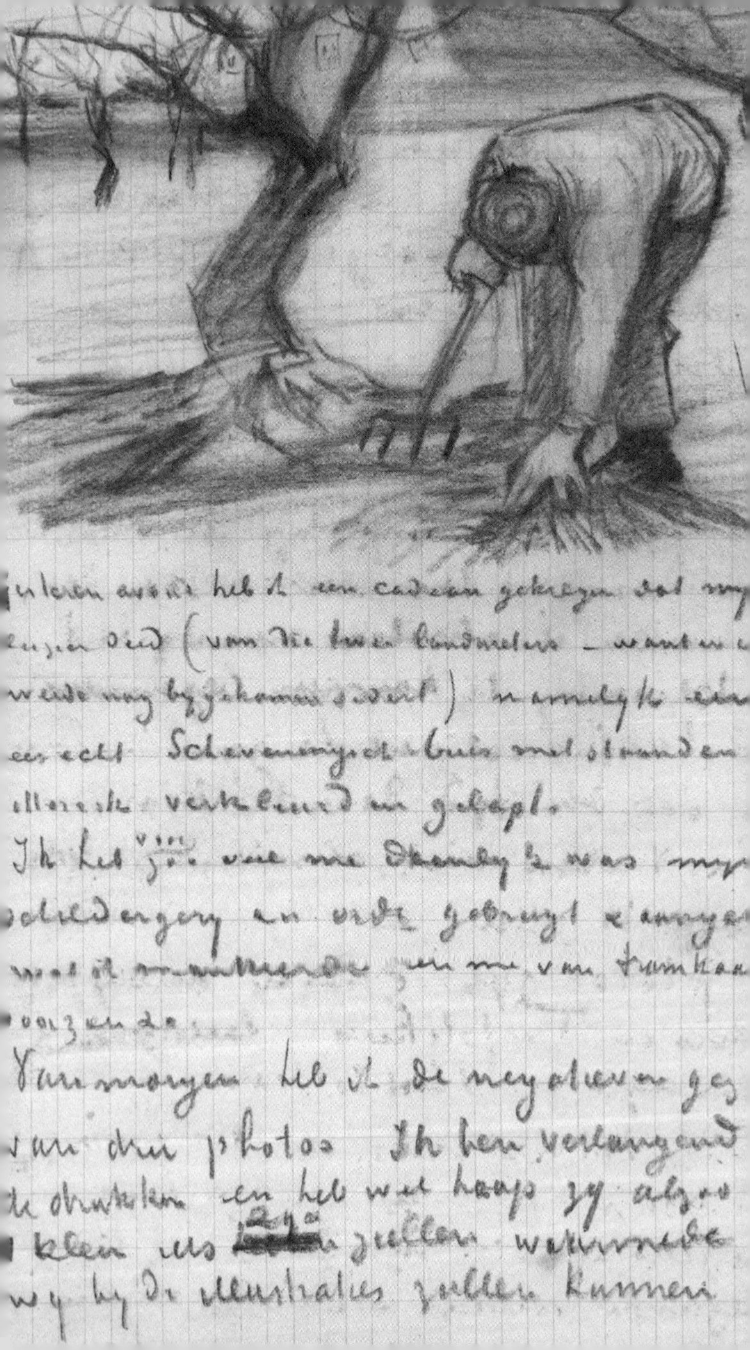

'When times are difficult we must give each other moral courage at the least, so that we don't give up when trials come.

'And if we can preserve our serenity, there's hope of achieving something good that stands firmly on its feet.'

*To Theo van Gogh*
*on or about Friday, 13 July 1883*
*The Hague*

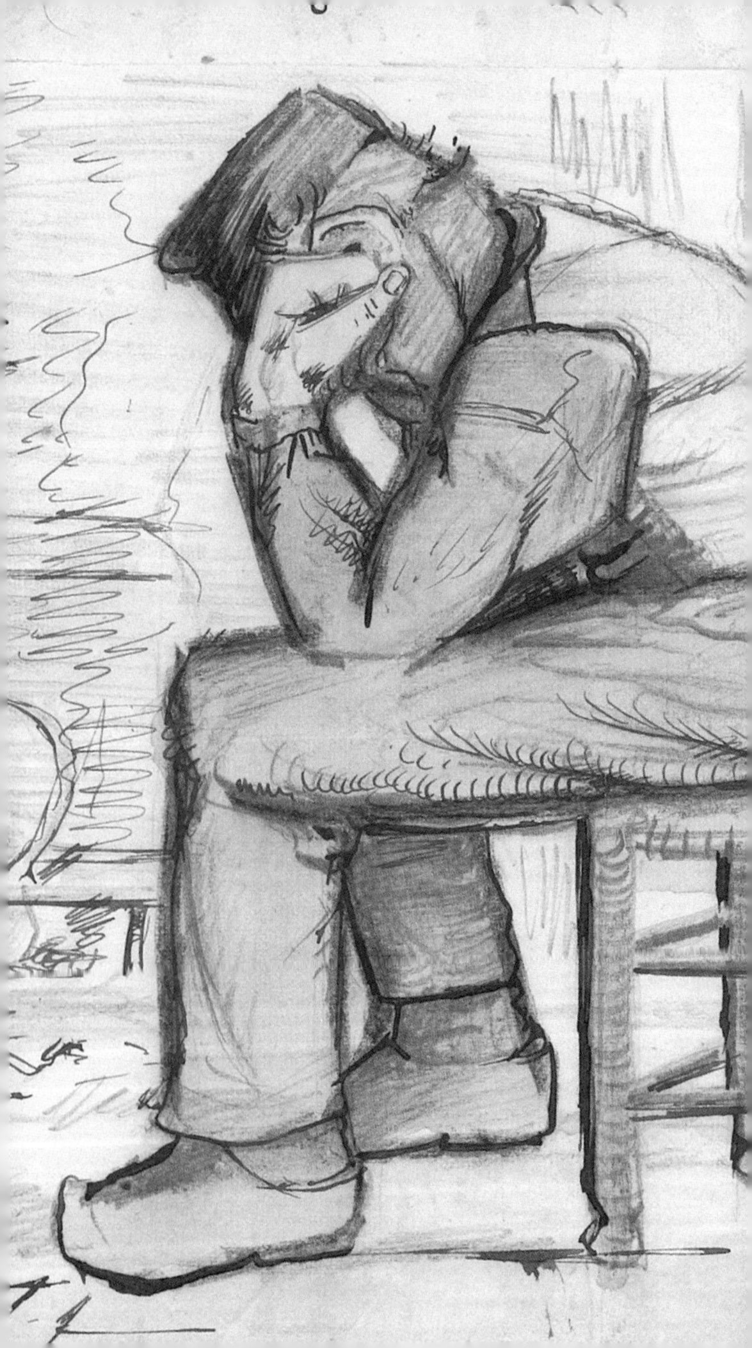

'… one mustn't begin by despairing; even if one loses here and there, and even if one sometimes feels a sort of decline, the point is nevertheless to revive and have courage, even though things don't turn out as one first thought. … I think principles are good and worth the effort only when they develop into deeds, and I think it's good to reflect and to try to be conscientious, because that makes a person's will to work more resolute and turns the various actions into a whole.'

*To Theo van Gogh*
*Sunday, 22 October 1882*
*The Hague*

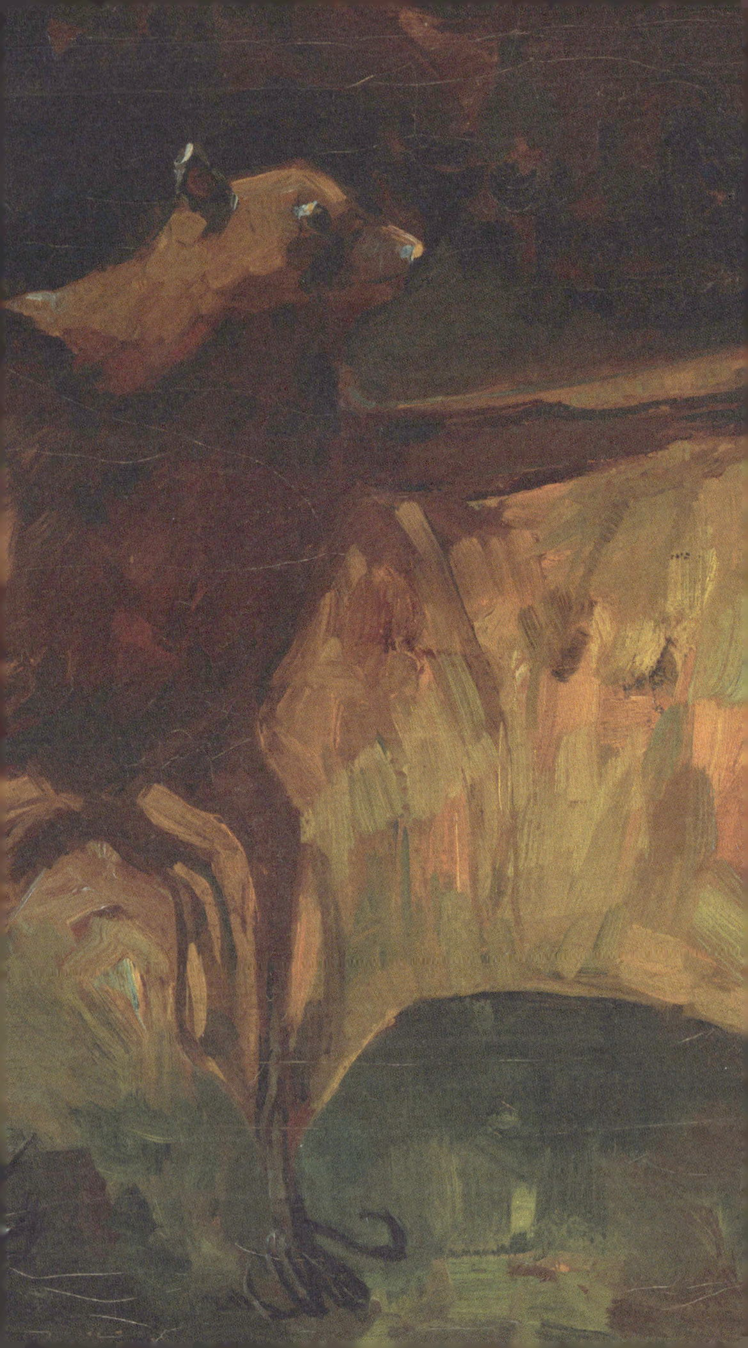

'When an apple is ripe, all it takes is a
gentle breeze to make it fall from the tree,
it's also like that here. I've certainly done
things that were in some way very wrong,
and so have little to say.

'And now, old boy, so far I'm really rather
in the dark about what I should do, but we
must try and keep hope and courage alive.'

*To Theo van Gogh*
*Monday, 10 January 1876*
*Paris*

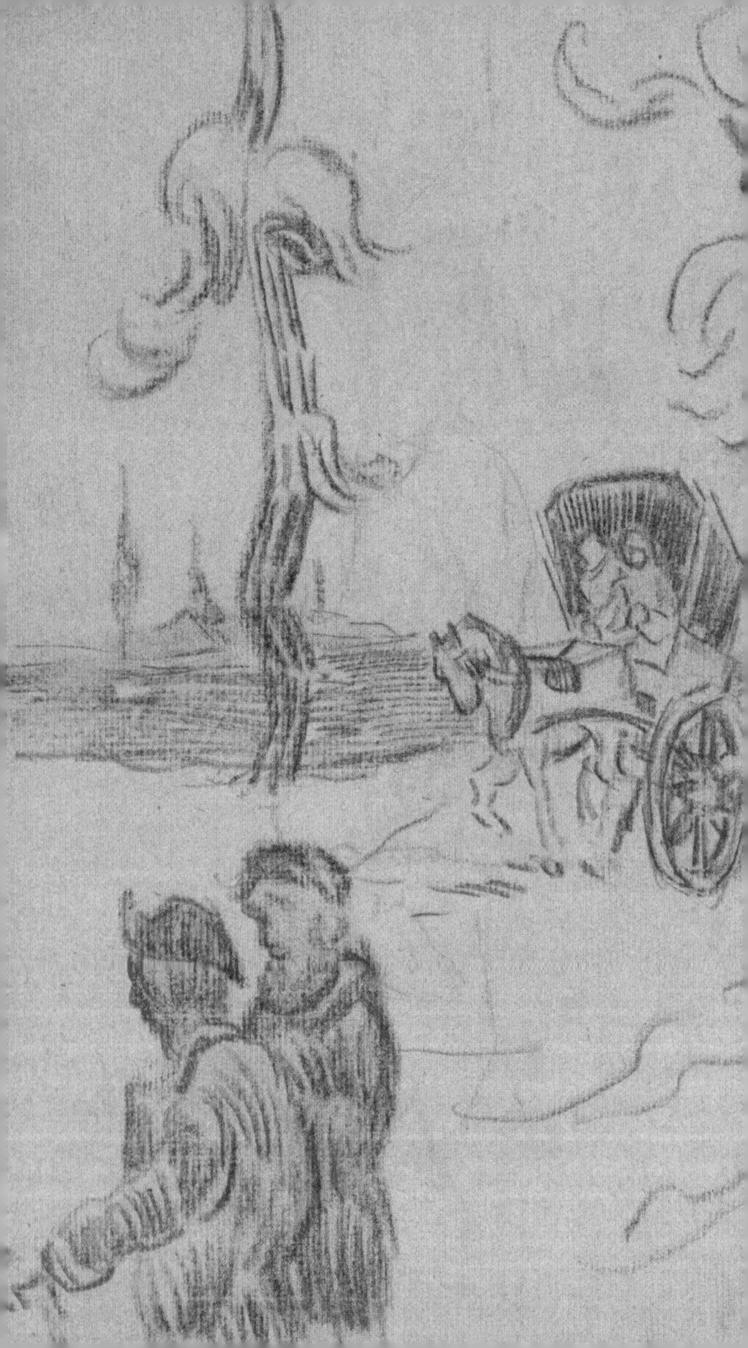

'I've suffered a great many "petty miseries of human life", which, if they were written down in a book, could perhaps serve to amuse some people, though they can hardly be considered pleasant if one experiences them oneself. Nonetheless, up to now I've been glad that I left the resignation or "how-*not*-to-do-it" method to those who prefer it and, as for myself, plucked up a little courage. You understand that in cases like this it's surprisingly difficult to know what one can, may and must do. But "wandering we find our way", and not by sitting still.'

*To Theo van Gogh*
*Thursday, 3 November 1881*
*Etten*

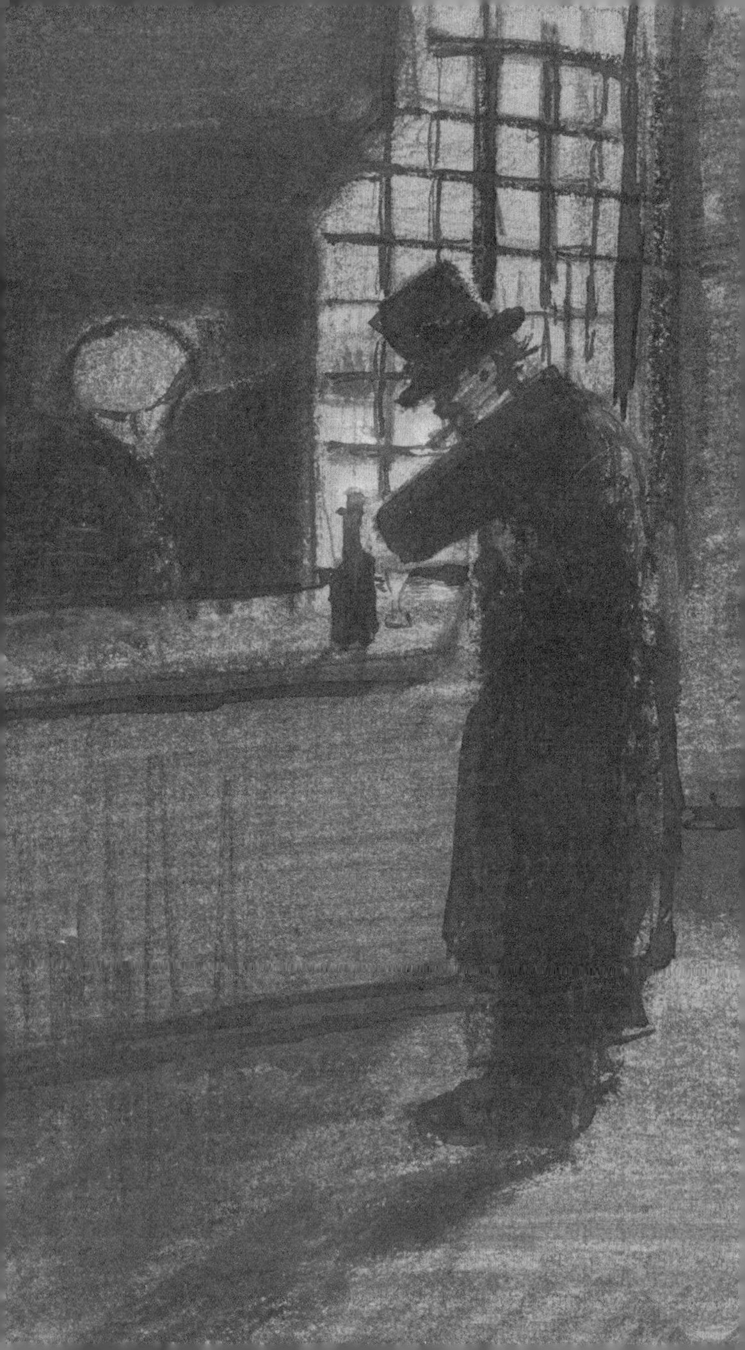

'We must have no illusions, but prepare ourselves for being misunderstood, despised and vilified, and under all that, even when it gets much worse than it is now, we'll have to hold on to courage and fervour. I believe we'll do well to keep our attention fixed on the work ...'

*To Anthon van Rappard*
*Wednesday, 1 November 1882*
*The Hague*

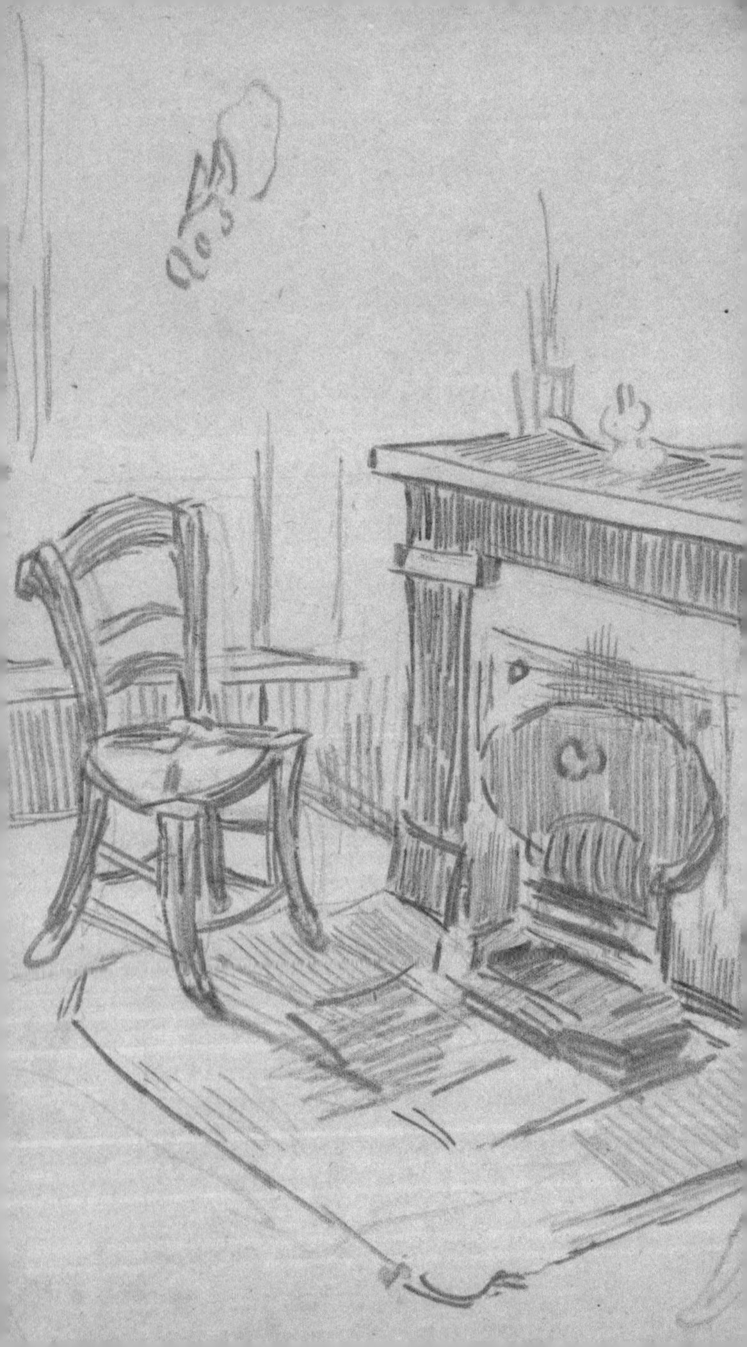

'If things stay quiet, we'll fight our fight here by working, and that may be just everyday and ordinary but it isn't easy either, and courage and energy are needed to set about it vigorously and keep it up.'

*To Theo van Gogh*
*Tuesday, 18 July 1882*
*The Hague*

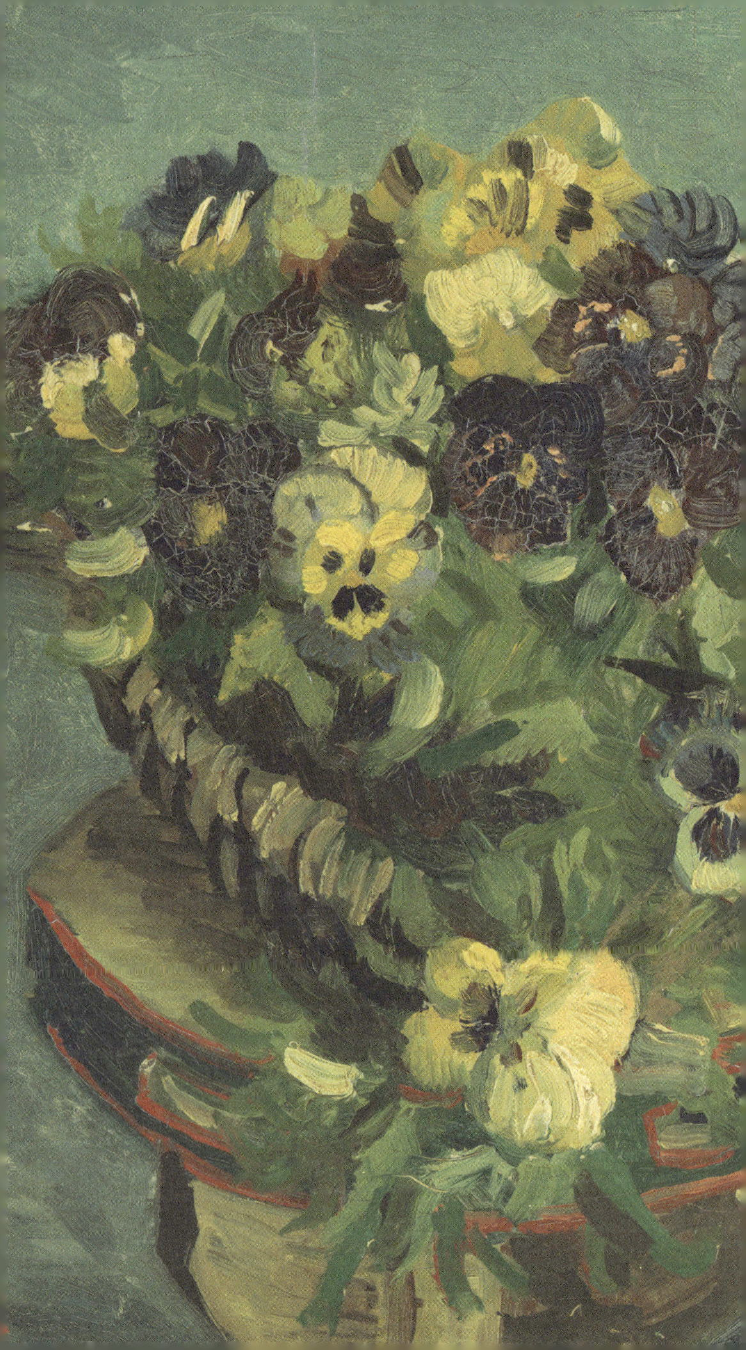

'– let's not forget that small emotions are the great captains of our lives, and that these we obey without knowing it. If it's still hard for me to regain courage over faults committed and to be committed, which would be my recovery, let's not forget from that moment on that neither our spleens and melancholies nor our feelings of good nature and good sense are our sole guides, and above all not our final custodians …'

*To Theo van Gogh*
*Sunday, 14 or Monday, 15 July 1889*
*Saint-Rémy-de-Provence*

# INTERACTION

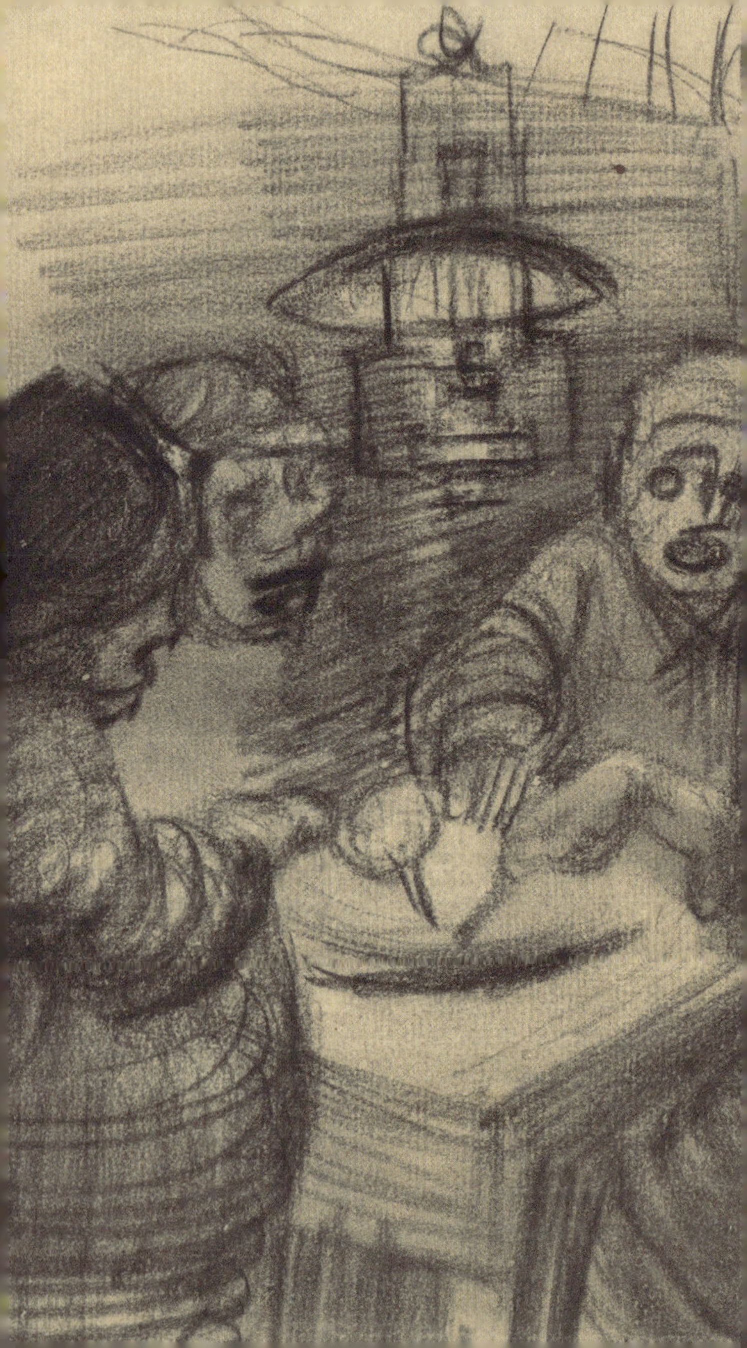

'Look, in my opinion all civility is based on kindness towards everyone, especially towards those we know – based on the need felt by anyone with a heart in his breast to mean something to others and to be of some use – on the need one ultimately has to live with others and not alone. It's for that that I do my best, I draw not to annoy people but to amuse them, or to draw their attention to things that are worth looking at and which not everyone knows.'

*To Theo van Gogh*
*on or about Sunday, 23 April 1882*
*The Hague*



ADVICE FOR
THE SOUL

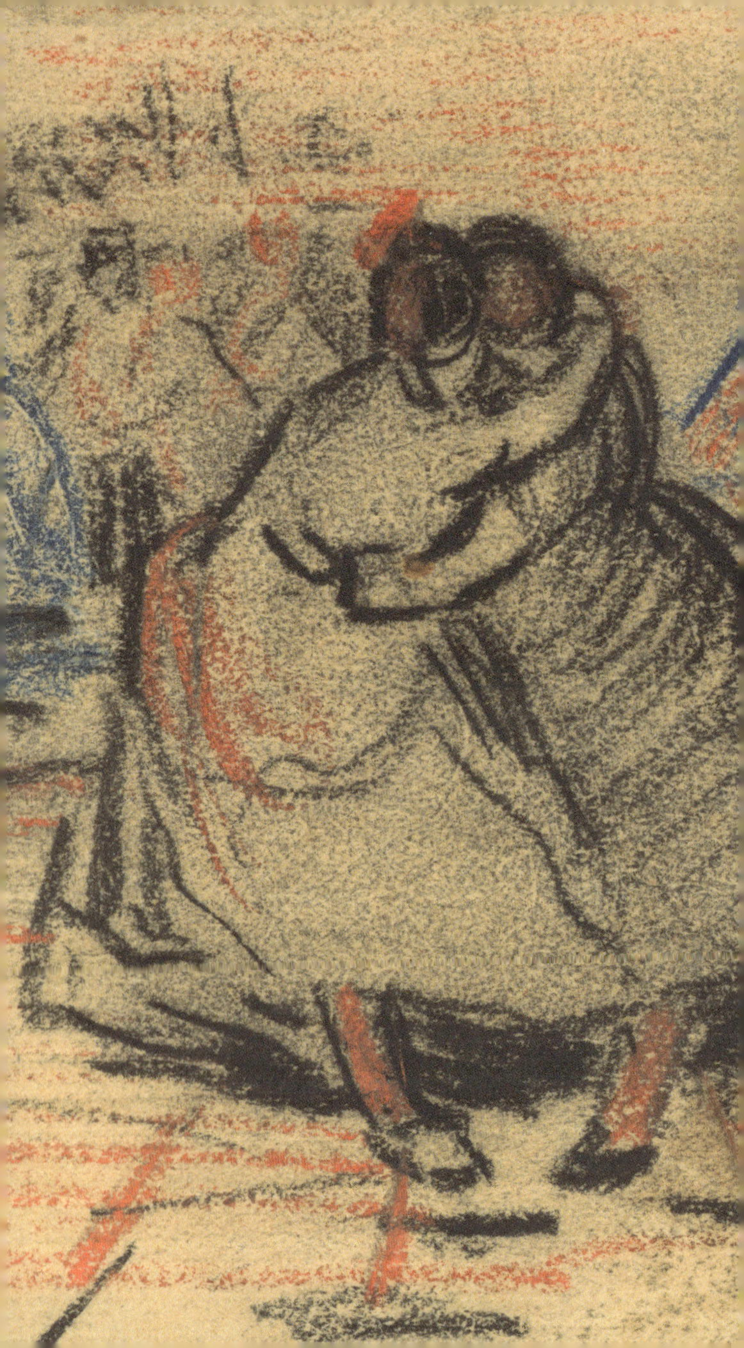

'I still often go to the dance halls to
see these women's heads and sailors'
or soldiers' heads. One pays 20 or 30
centimes to go in and drinks a glass of
beer – for there's little drinking – and
can amuse oneself exceedingly for a whole
evening – at least I can – watching the
folks' high spirits.'

*To Theo van Gogh*
*Monday, 28 December 1885*
*Antwerp*

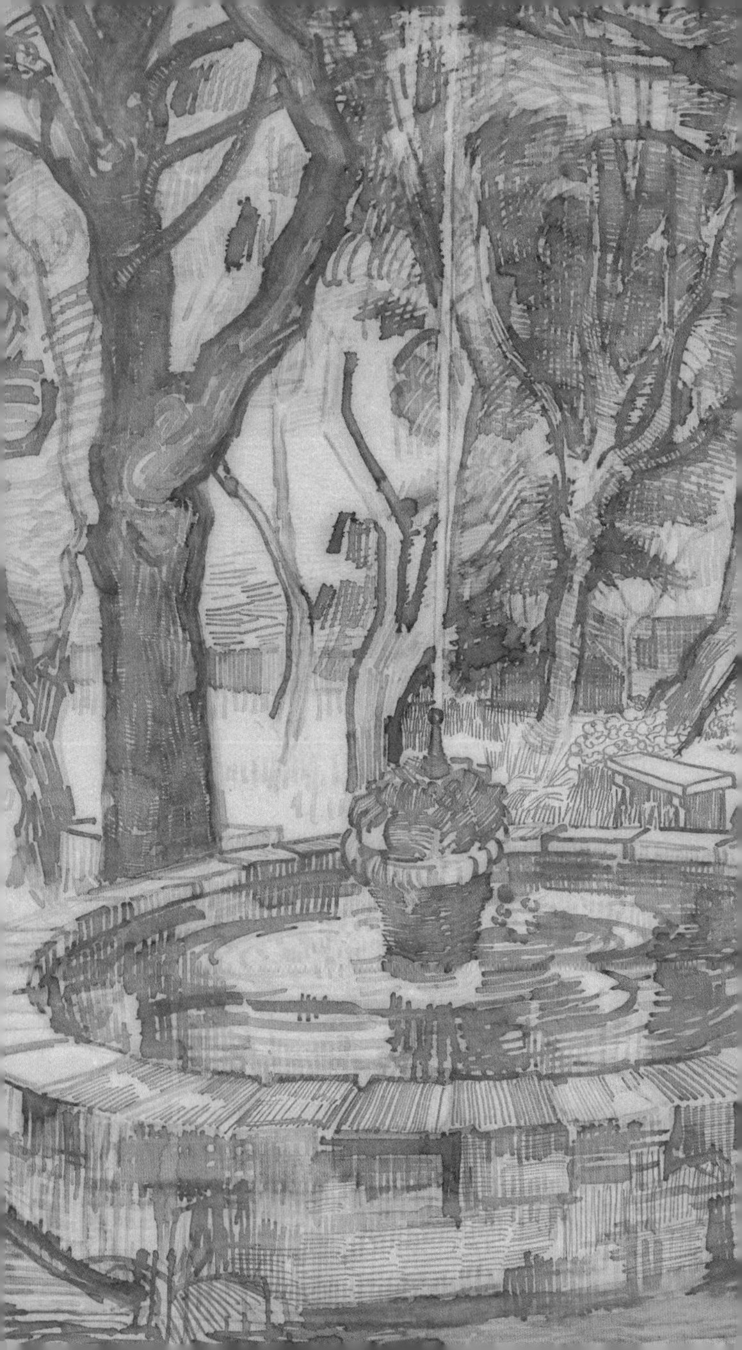

'When you say in your last letter "what
a riddle there is in nature", I echo your
words. Life in the abstract is already
a riddle, reality turns it into a riddle
within a riddle.

'And who are we to solve it? All the same,
we ourselves form a particle of it, of
the society of which we ask, Where is it
going, to the devil or to God?'

*To Theo van Gogh*
*Sunday, 10 December 1882*
*The Hague*

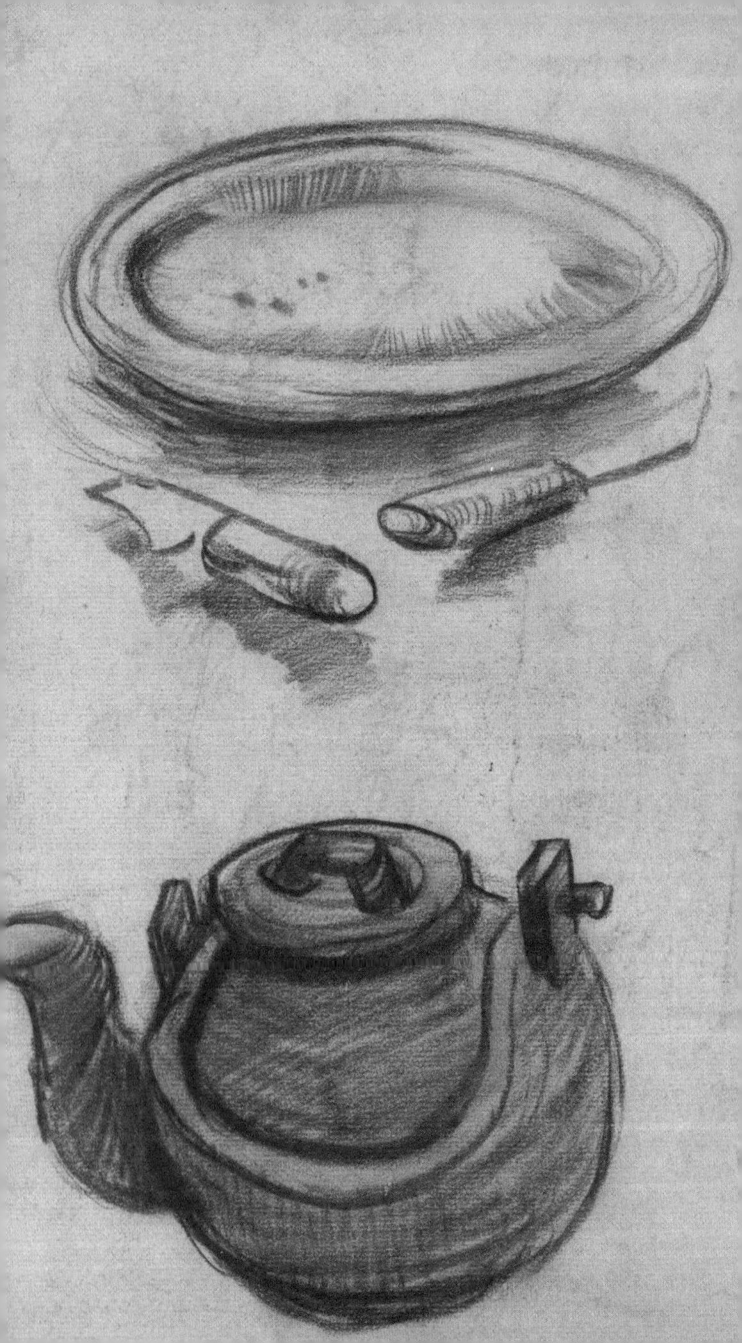

'But I do know this, that even if
I occasionally address you in what
are possibly coarse and harsh terms,
I nevertheless feel such warm sympathy
for you that you will surely see and feel
when calmly reading or re-reading my
letter – the person who speaks to me
thus is not my enemy. And knowing this,
is it then so utterly unbearable for you
to swallow somewhat coarse and harsh
expressions even if they later appear to
be less coarse and harsh than you at
first thought?'

*To Anthon van Rappard*
*Saturday, 12 November 1881*
*Etten*

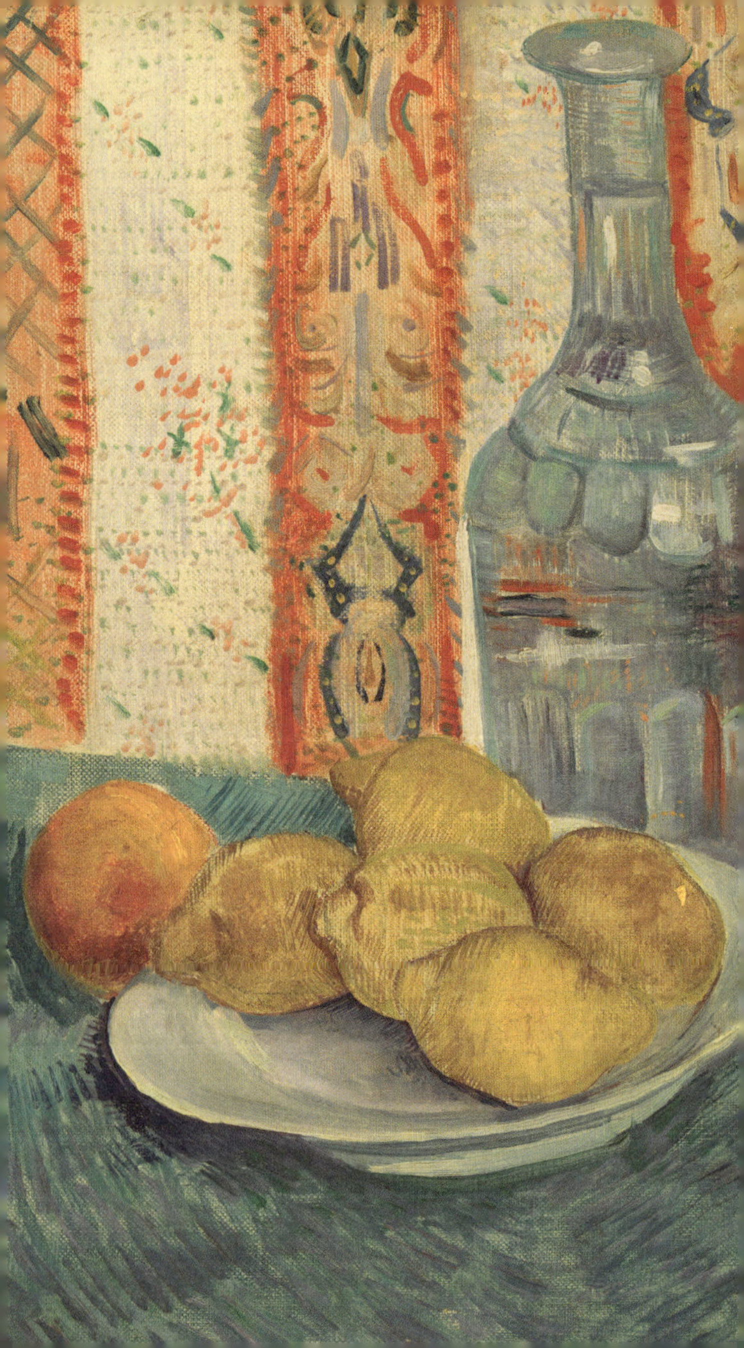

'Because it's better to take a long look
at it before judging so categorically,
and to reflect, reflection making us
see in ourselves, when there's a falling
out, as many faults on our own side as
in our adversary, and in him as many
justifications as we might desire for
ourselves.'

*To Emile Bernard*
*about December 1887*
*Paris*

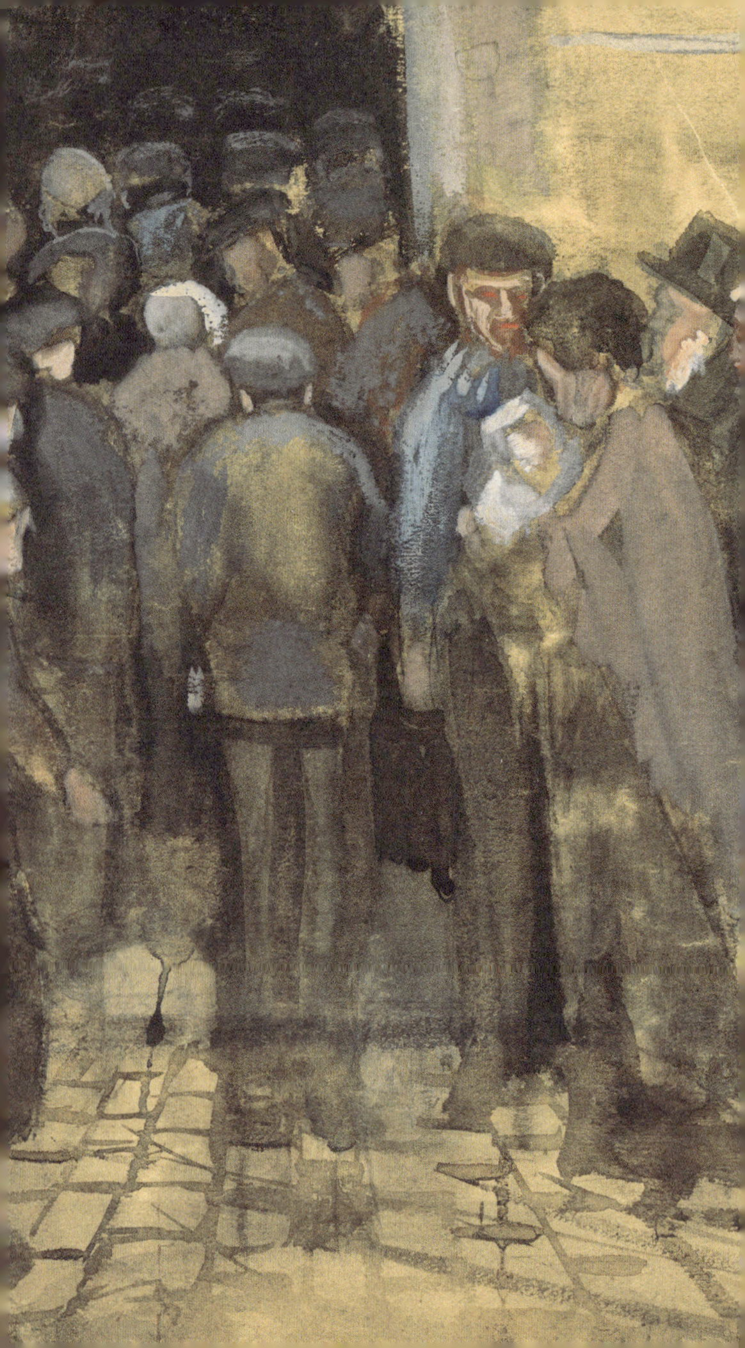

'And then there's the fact that the material difficulties of the painter's life make collaboration, union among painters, desirable …

'By safeguarding their material life, by liking each other as pals instead of getting at each other's throats, painters would be happier and anyway less ridiculous, less foolish and less guilty.

'However, I don't insist, knowing that life carries us along so fast that we don't have the time to discuss and act simultaneously. That's why at present, while the union exists only very incompletely, we're sailing on the high seas in our small and wretched boats, isolated on the great waves of our time.'

*To Emile Bernard*
*between Tuesday, 17 and Friday, 20 July 1888*
*Arles*



ADVICE FOR
THE SOUL

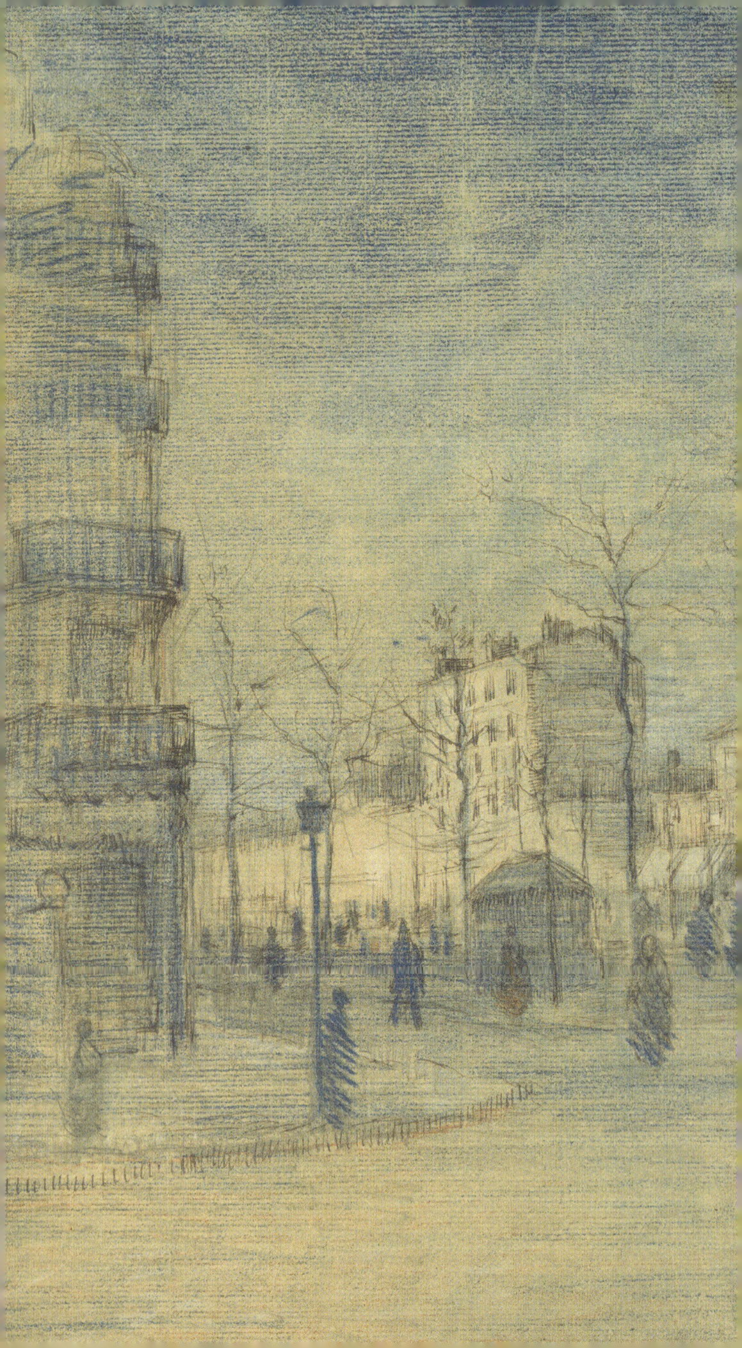

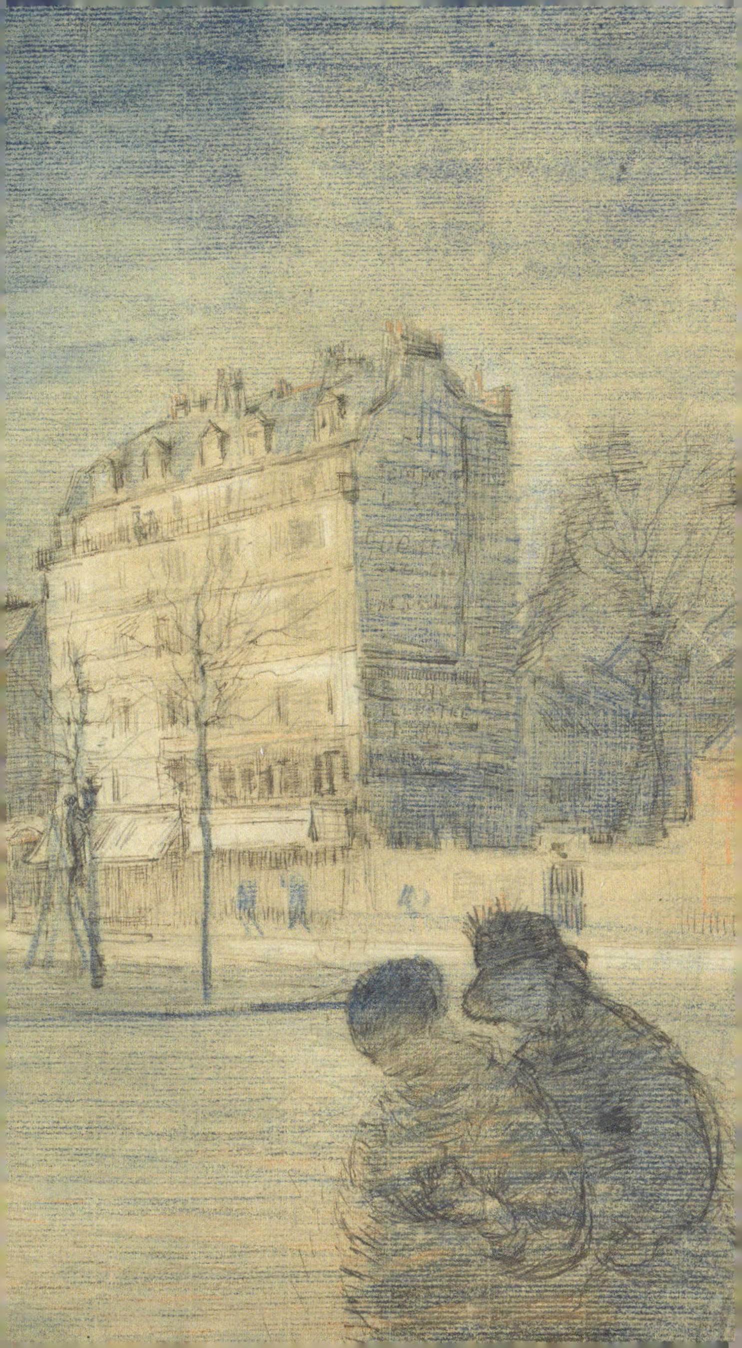

'Since I am here in Paris I have very often thought of your self and work. You will remember that I liked your colour, your ideas on art and literature and I add, most of all, your personality.

'I have already before now thought that I ought to let you know what I was doing, where I was.

'But what refrained me was that I find living in Paris is much dearer than in Antwerp and not knowing what your circumstances are I dare not say Come over to Paris, without warning you that it costs one dearer than Antwerp and that if poor, one has to suffer many things. As you may imagine. But on the other hand there is more chance of selling.



ADVICE FOR
THE SOUL

'There is also a good chance of exchanging pictures with other artists.

'In one word, with much energy, with a sincere personal feeling of colour in nature I would say an artist can get on here notwithstanding the many obstructions. And I intend remaining here still longer.'

*To Horace Mann Livens*
*September or October 1886*
*Paris*

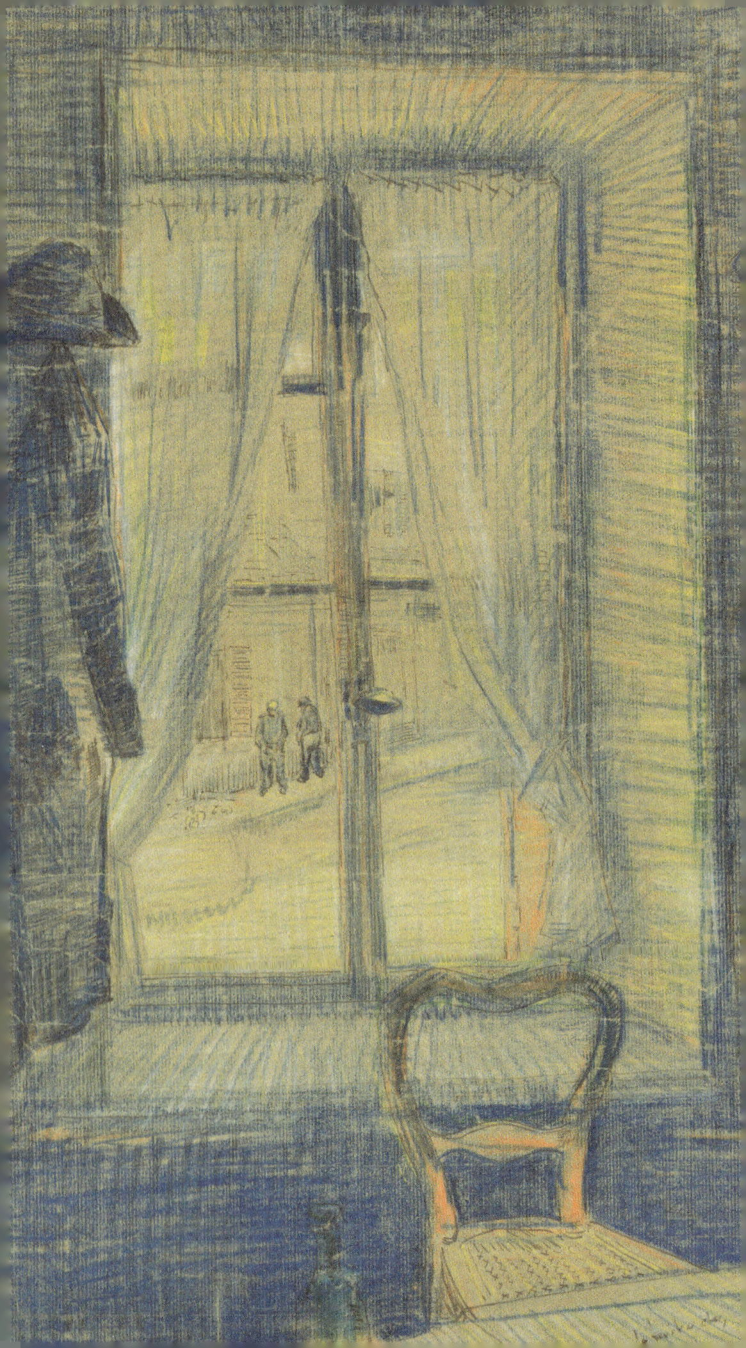

'Sometimes I start to believe that I'm gradually beginning to turn into a true cosmopolitan, meaning not a Dutchman, Englishman or Frenchman, but simply a *man*. With the world as my mother country, meaning that tiny spot in the world where we're set down.'

*To Caroline van Stockum-Haanebeek*
*Monday, 9 February 1874*
*London*

# PURPOSE

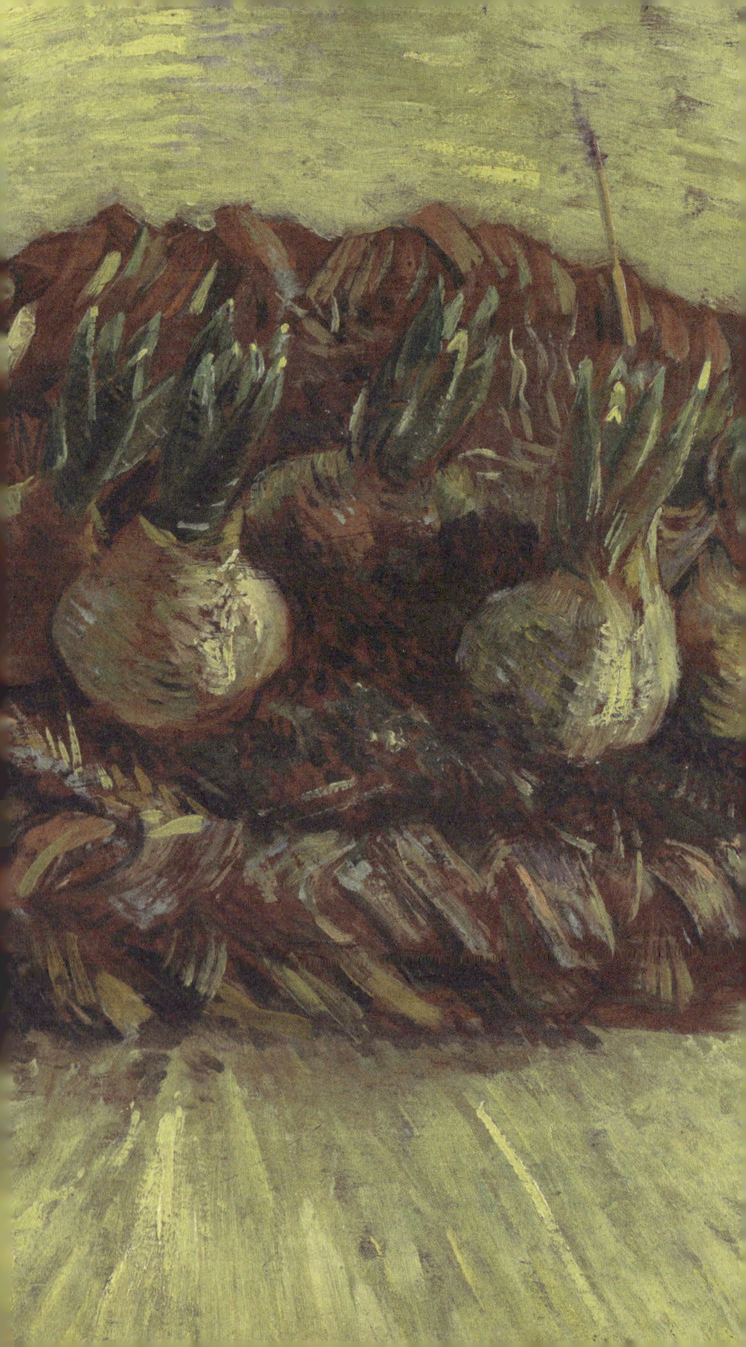

'Even though one seeks with the expectation of finding, finding is a complete surprise nonetheless.'

*To Theo van Gogh*
*Monday, 7 November 1881*
*Etten*

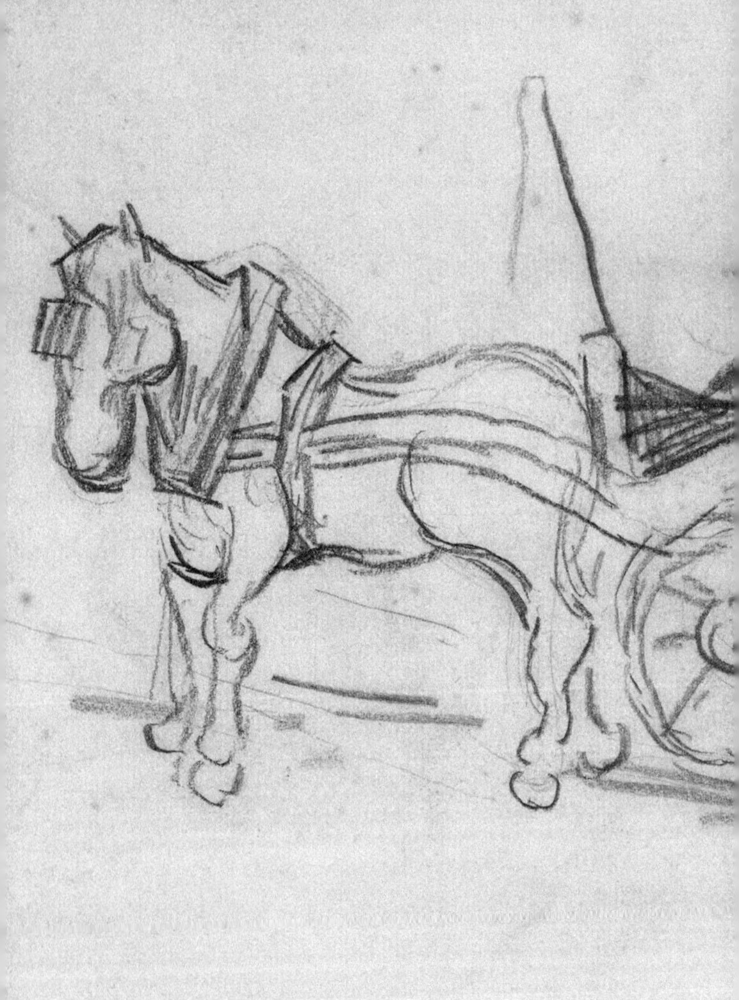

'Now I'm going through a similar period of struggle and despondency, of patience and impatience, of hope and desolation. But I must plod on and anyway, after a while I'll understand more …

'If it were that easy, one wouldn't take any pleasure in it.'

*To Theo van Gogh*
*Sunday, 8 or Monday, 9 January 1882*
*The Hague*

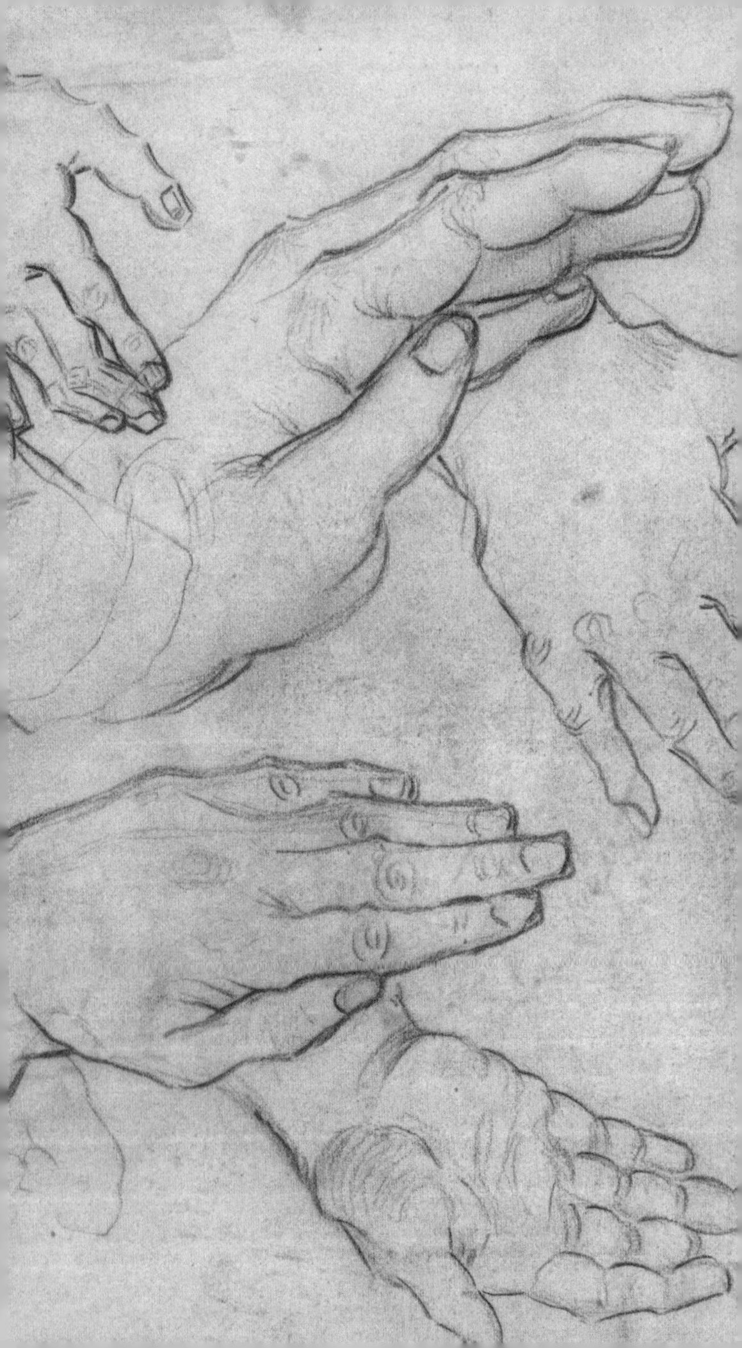

'Do right and don't look back, and things will turn out well.'

*To Theo van Gogh*
*Thursday, 30 April 1874*
*London*

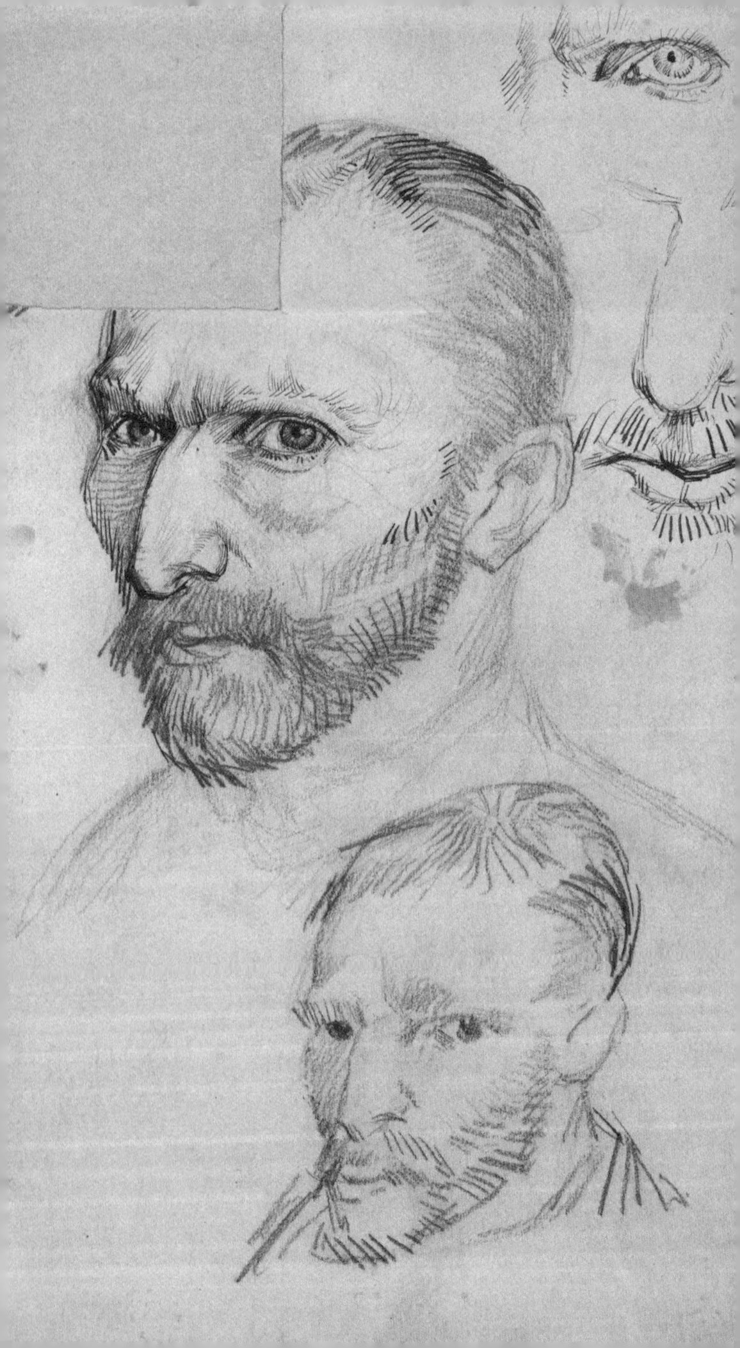

'Certainly it's presumptuous to feel sure
of one's success, and yet one may believe:
my inner struggle will not be in vain, and
I want to fight it; despite all my own
weaknesses and faults I want to fight it as
best I can.

'Even if I fall down 99 times, the hundredth
time, too, I'll get up! … What artist hasn't
struggled and toiled, and what other way
is there than struggling and toiling to find
firm ground beneath one's feet?'

*To Theo van Gogh*
*Saturday, 19 November 1881*
*Etten*

e ne puis être sûr qu'[...]
au même endroit cette année ( cep[en...]
elles y viennent depuis plusieurs années.
Perruchot doit connaître l'adresse en t[...]
C'est peut être une illusion que je
fais mais — je ne puis m'empê-
d'y penser et peut être cela leur fer[a...]
et à toi aussi si tu les connais.
Écoutes — je ferai tout mon pos[sible]
de l'envoyer de nouveau des[...]
pour Dordrecht
J'ai fait cette semaine deux natur[es]
mortes.

une cafetière en fer émaillé bleu une tasse (à gau[che]
de roi et or un pot à lait carrelé bleu pâle et blan[c]
une tasse — à droite blanche à dessins bleu et orang[e]
une assiette de terre jaune gris un pot en
ou majolique bleu avec dessins rouges verts bru[ns]
enfin 2 oranges et 3 citrons la table est
d'une draperie bleue le fond est jaune ve[rt]
donc 6 bleus différents et 4 ou 5 jaunes et orangé
L'autre nature morte est le pot de majolique avec
fleurs sauvages

'Success is sometimes the outcome of a
whole string of failures.'

*To Theo van Gogh*
*on or about Sunday, 1 October 1882*
*The Hague*

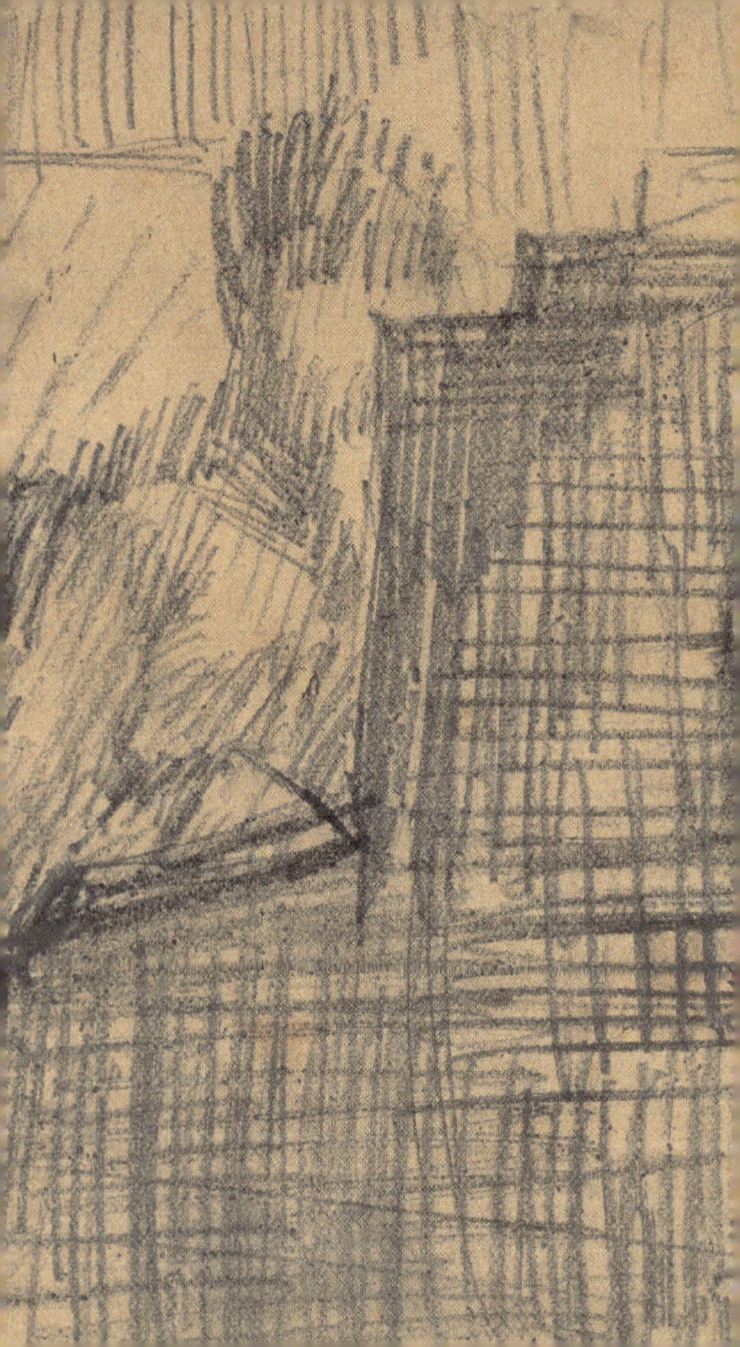

'My mood varies, of course, but nonetheless I have a certain average serenity. I have a certain *faith* in art, a certain *trust* that it's a powerful current that drives a person – although he has to cooperate – to a haven, and in any case I consider it such a great happiness if a person has found his work that I don't count myself among the unfortunate.'

*To Theo van Gogh*
*Sunday, 11 March 1883*
*The Hague*

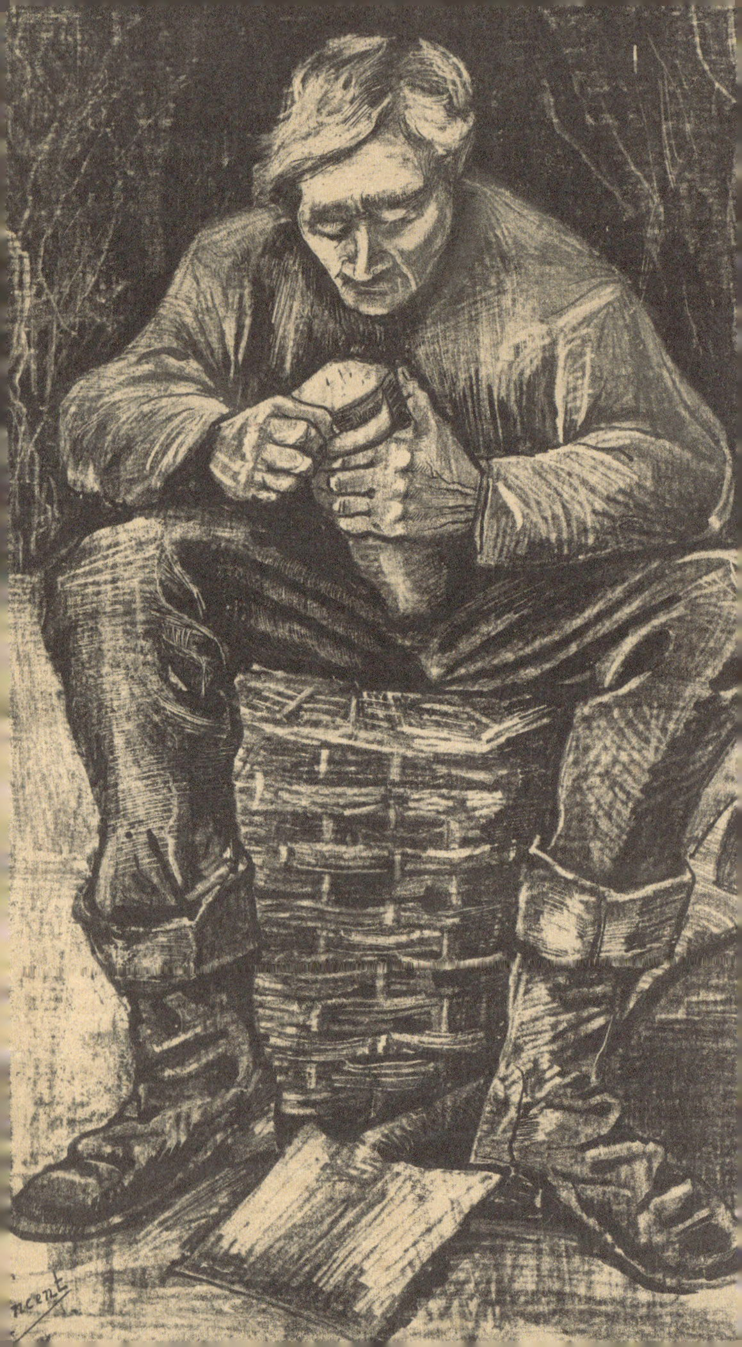

'*… let's keep up each other's enthusiasm,* and let's encourage each other, as far as we can, to carry on working. Not in the direction of pleasing dealers or the ordinary art lovers but in the direction of manly strength, truth, loyalty, honesty.'

*To Anthon van Rappard*
*on or about Wednesday, 21 March 1883*
*The Hague*

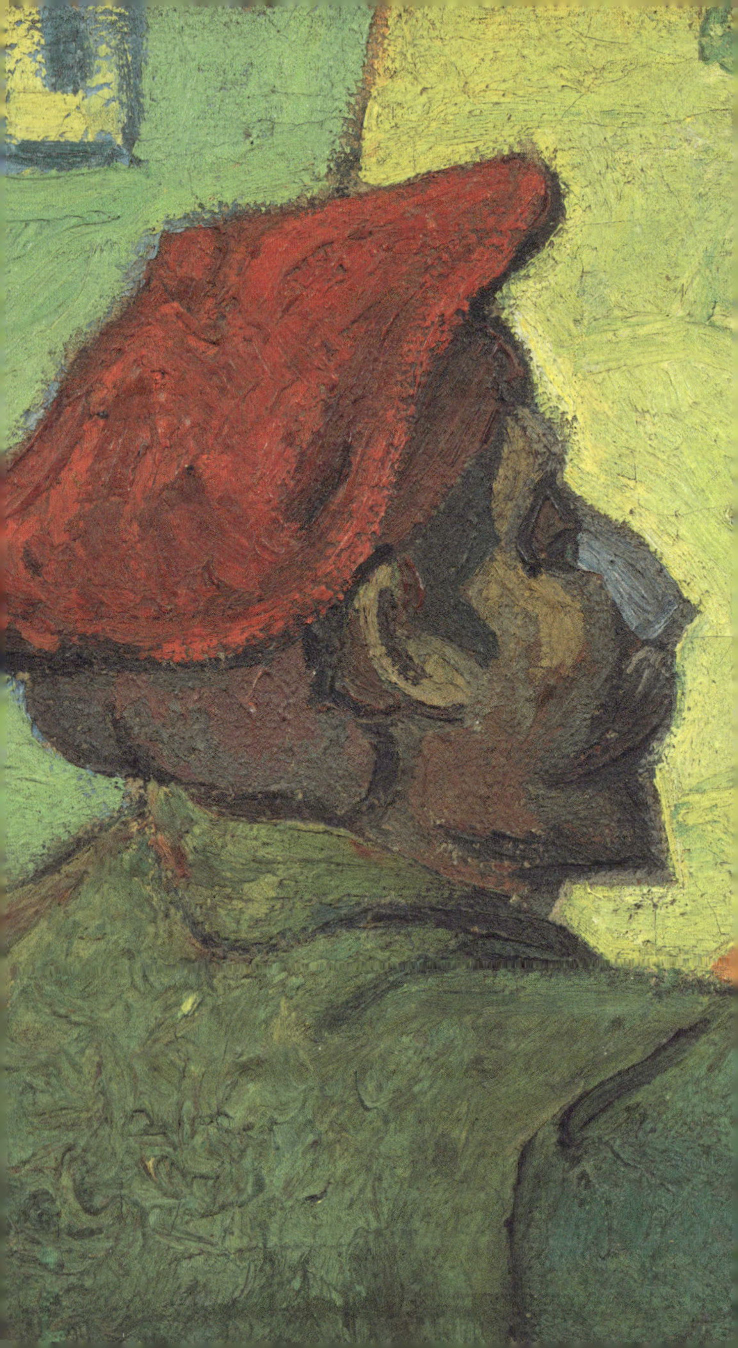

'I believe that it would make an enormous
difference to me if Gauguin was here,
because the days pass now without saying
a word to anyone. Ah, well. In any case, his
letter gave me tremendous pleasure.

'Being too long alone in the country you
become dull-witted, and not just yet – but
this winter, I could become sterile from
that. Now this danger will no longer exist
if he comes, because we won't be short
of ideas.

'If work goes well and if we don't lack guts,
there's the hope of seeing very interesting
years in the future.'

*To Theo van Gogh*
*Tuesday, 24 or Wednesday, 25 July 1888*
*Arles*

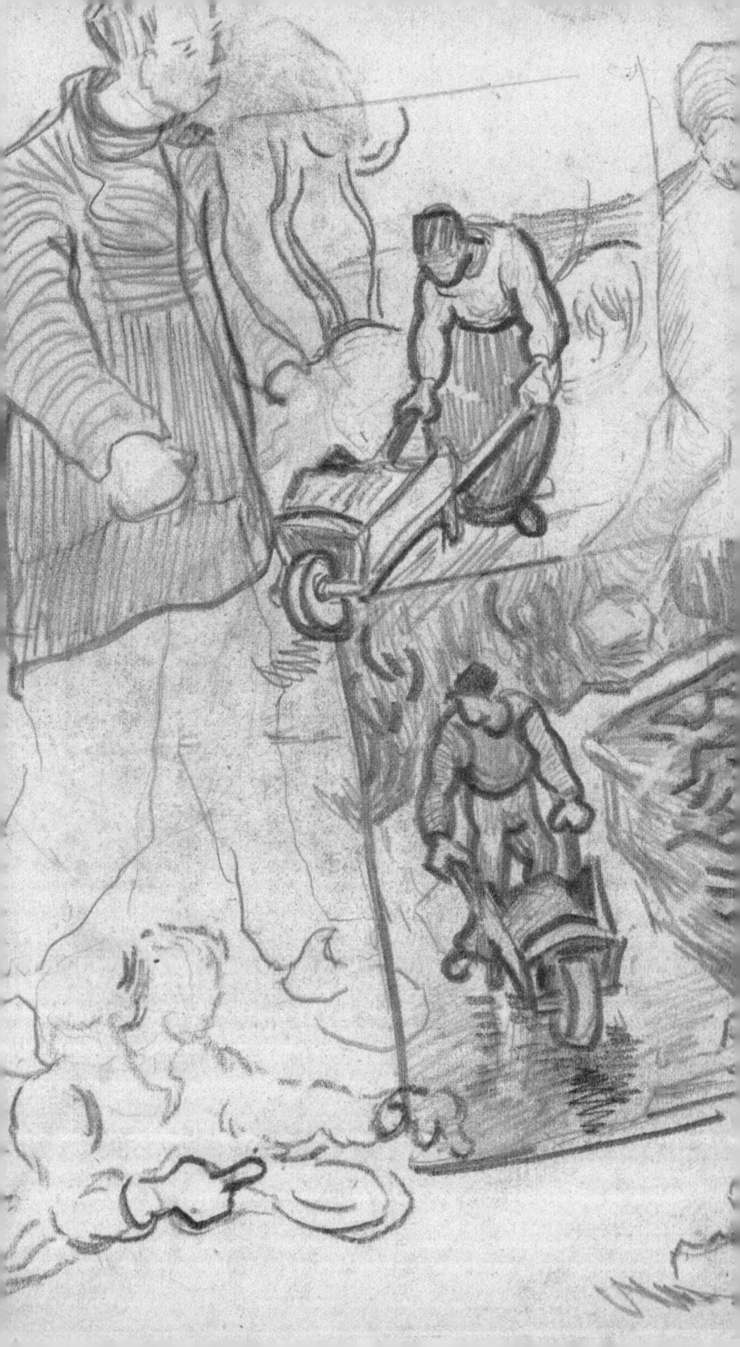

'One must work long and hard to arrive at the truthful. What I want and set as my goal is damned difficult, and yet I don't believe I'm aiming too high. I want to make drawings that *move* some people.'

*To Theo van Gogh*
*on or about Friday, 21 July 1882*
*The Hague*

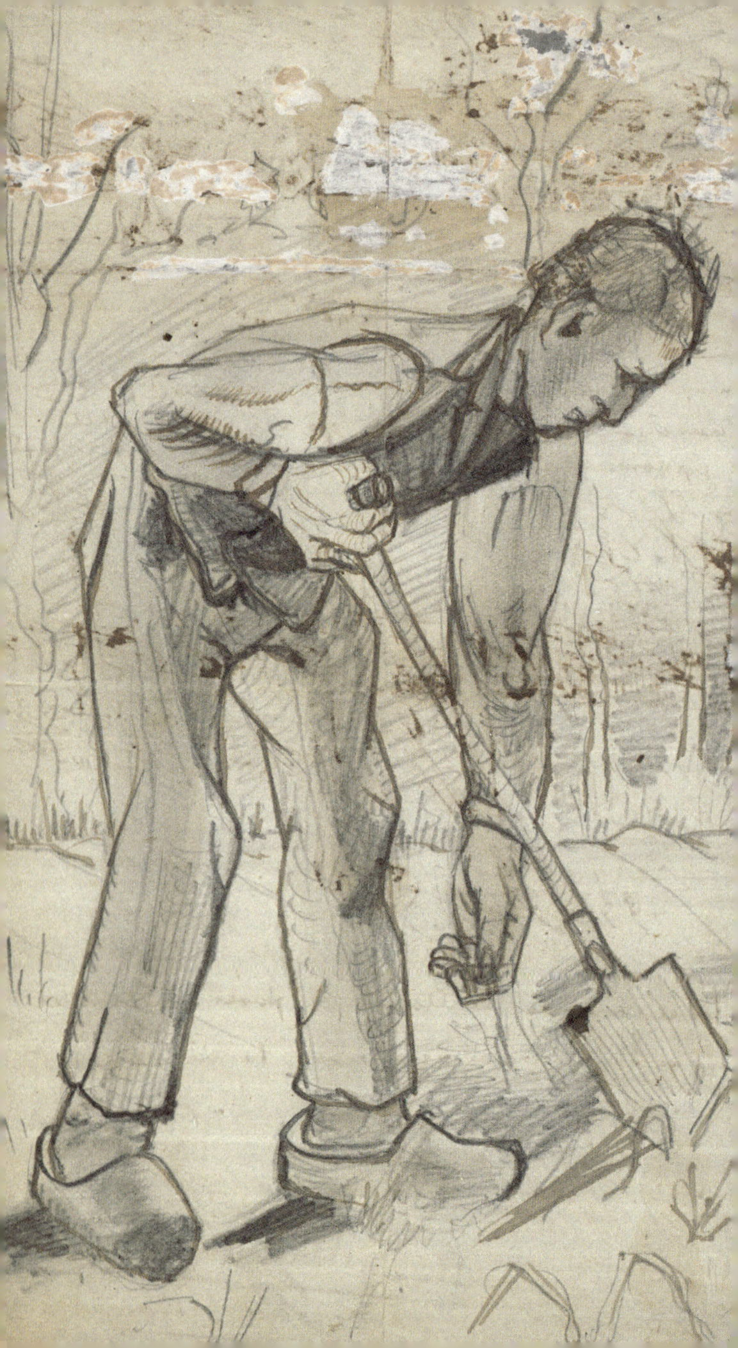

'Be in no doubt, though – the way to succeed is – to keep courage and patience, and to carry on working hard …'

*To Theo van Gogh*
*on or about Tuesday, 2 February 1886*
*Antwerp*

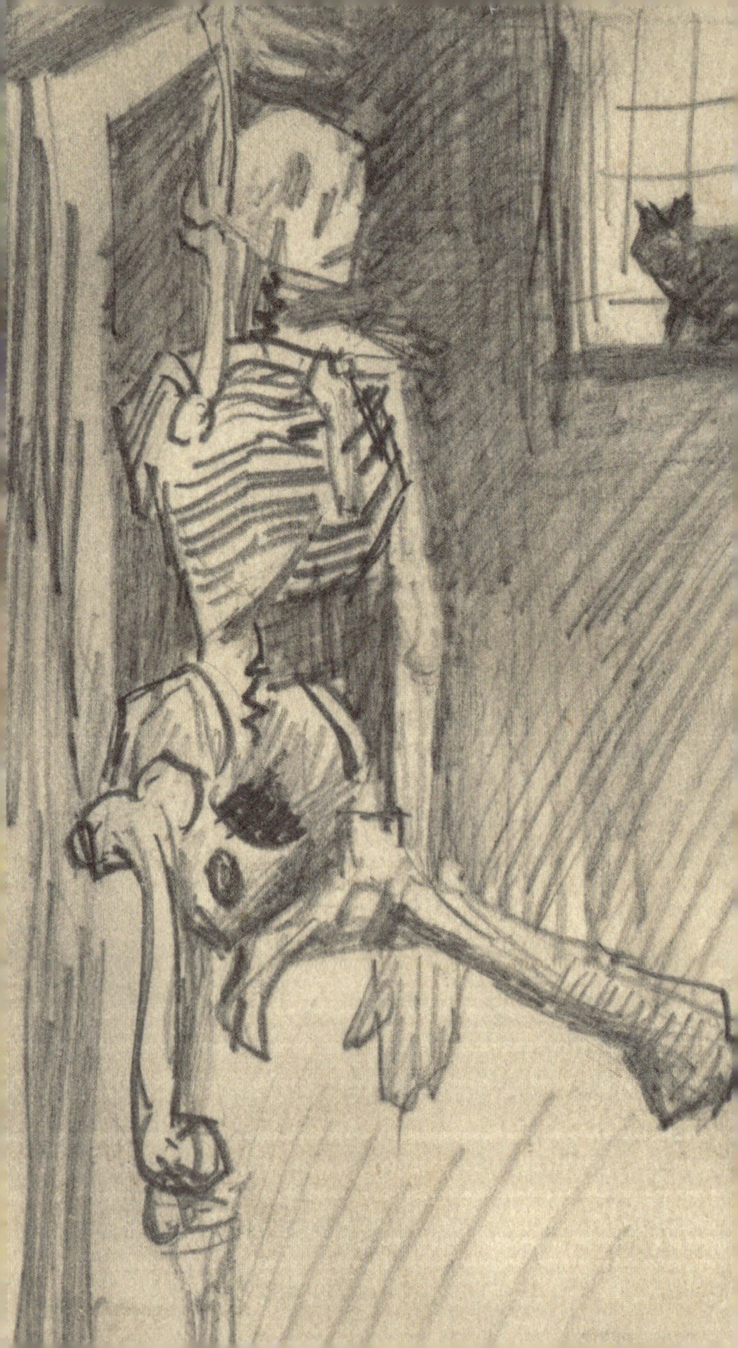

'I hope to do it better in time. I myself am very far from satisfied with this but, well, getting better must come through *doing* it and through trying.'

*To Theo van Gogh*
*Sunday, 26 and Monday, 27 November 1882*
*The Hague*

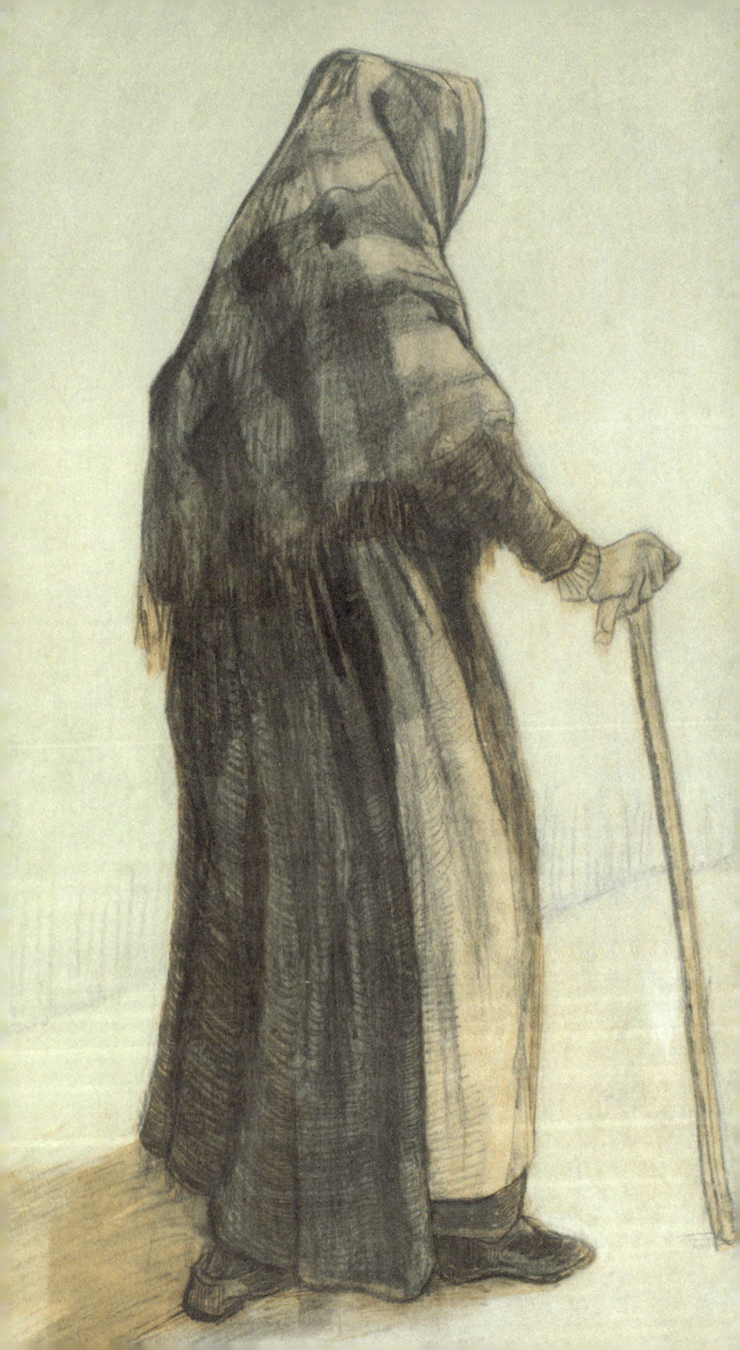

'In everything I often think of the words in Acts, "we came", we too must simply go on walking, try to get ahead, looking forward step by step to the goal and keeping it in sight, and when we have made an effort for a while in that way, "striving on", as Uncle Jan says, then we notice through one thing or another that we've come a long way.'

*To Theo van Gogh*
*Saturday, 18 August 1877*
*Amsterdam*

# FAMILY

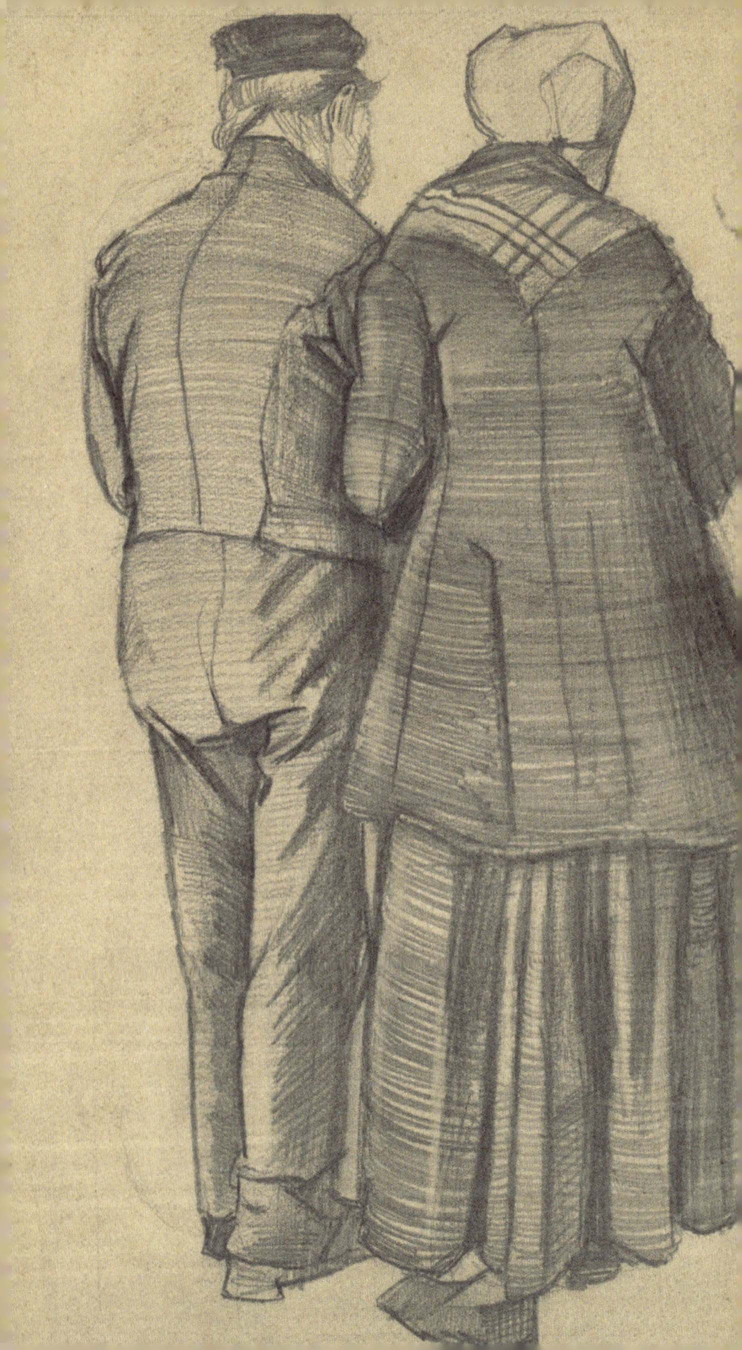

'For my part I desire so much to have the wisdom we see in our Father and Mother, in them to a greater extent than anywhere else, there is no family like ours, even, it seems to me, among good and noble people, among "the men of good will", like many painters and writers, none better than our Father.'

*To Theo van Gogh*
*Monday, 27 August 1877*
*Amsterdam*

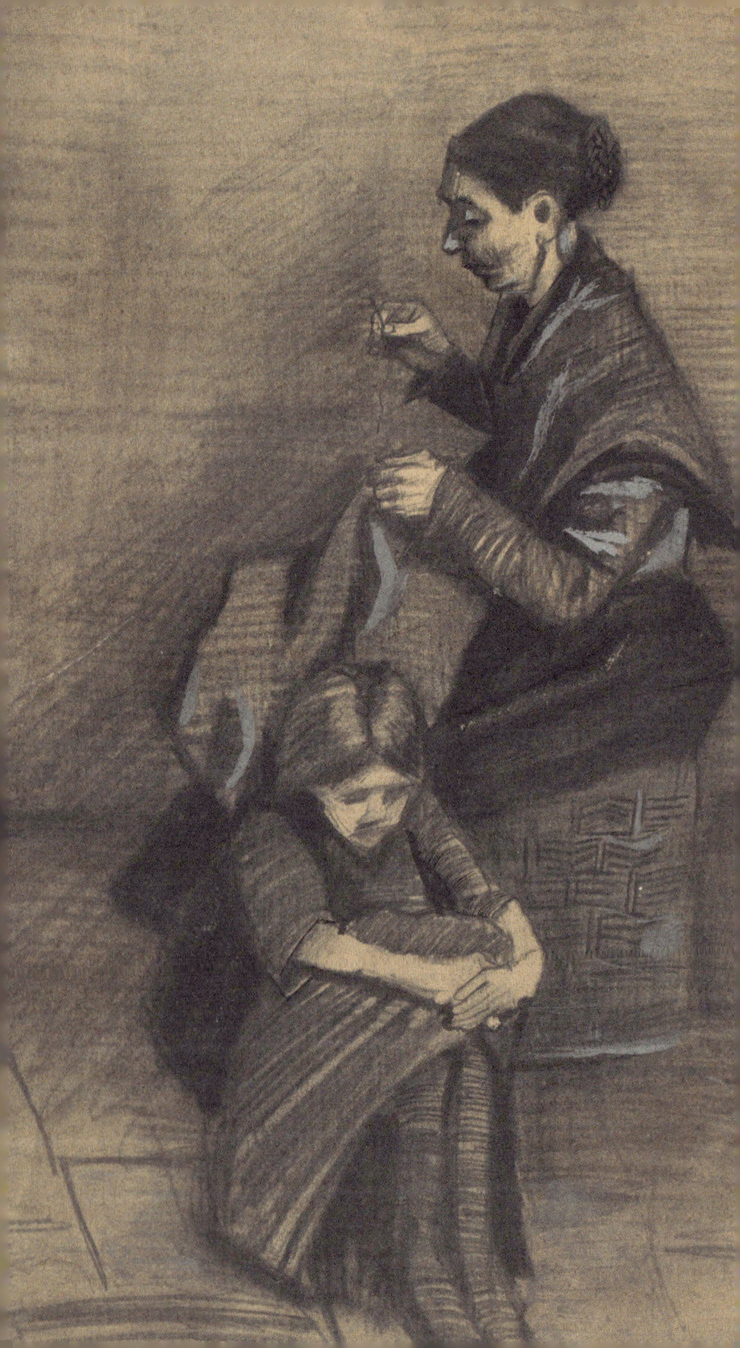

'May God grant that I find grace in the eyes of my Father and Mother and in the eyes of those who will come after me.'

*To Theo van Gogh*
*Saturday, 7 and Sunday, 8 October 1876*
*Isleworth*

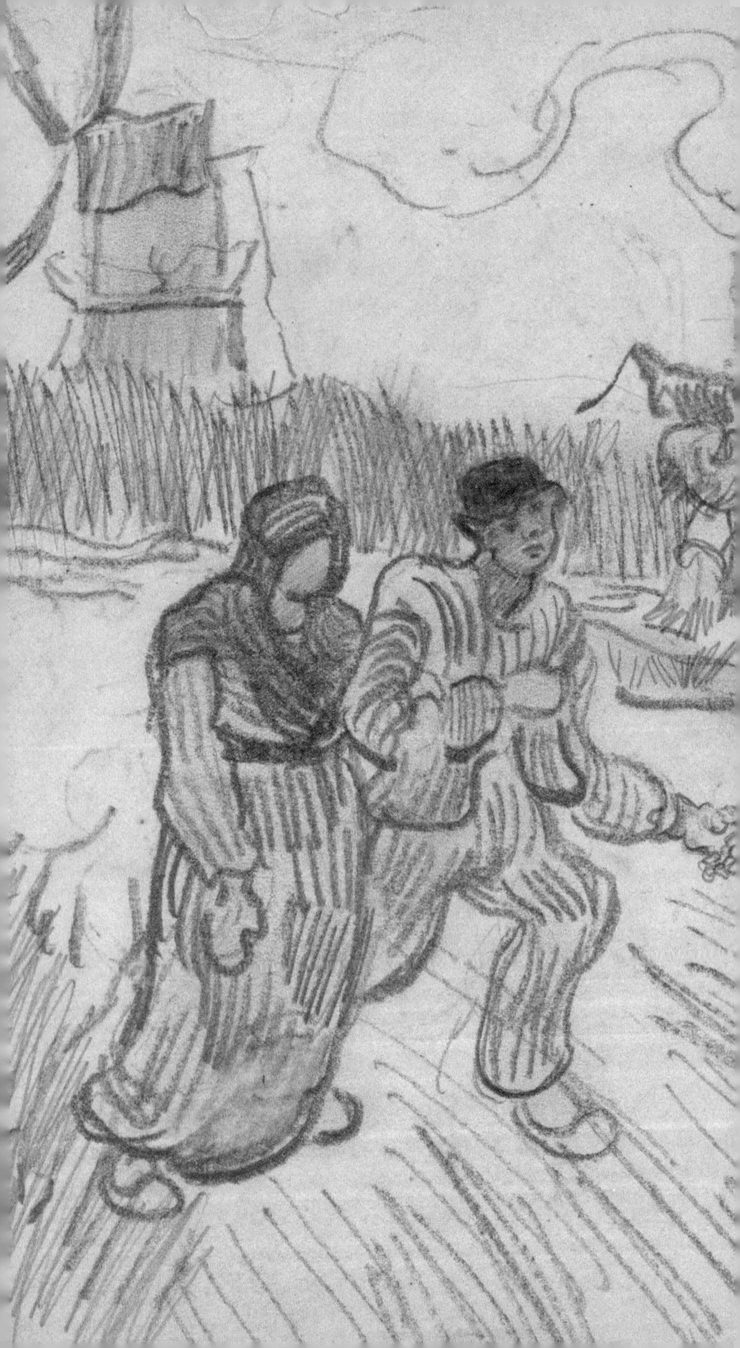

'When one lives with others and is bound by a feeling of affection one is aware that one has a reason for being, that one might not be entirely worthless and superfluous but perhaps good for one thing or another, considering that we need one another and are making the same journey as travelling companions.'

*To Theo van Gogh*
*between about Monday, 11 and Thursday, 14 August 1879*
*Cuesmes*

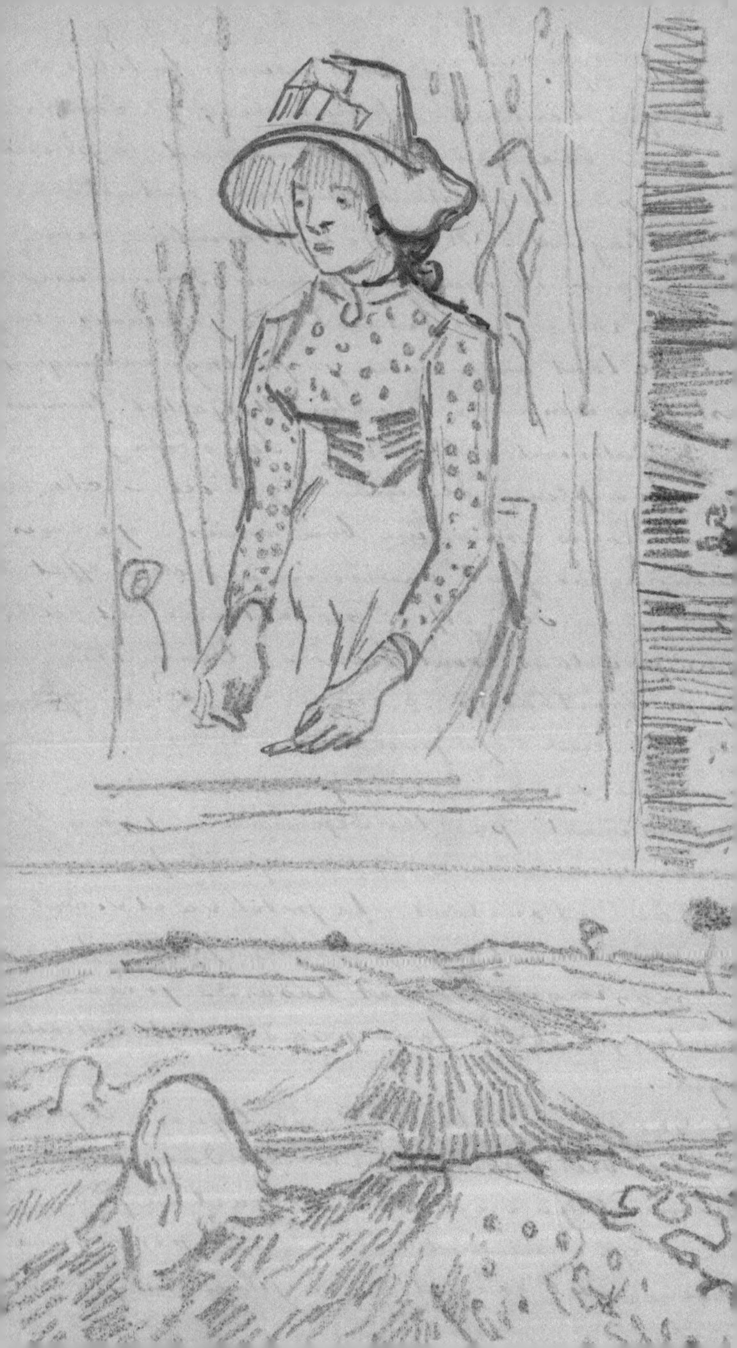

'I heard from Pa that you've already been sending me money without my knowing it, and in doing so are effectively helping me to get along. For this accept my heartfelt thanks. I have every confidence that you won't regret it; in this way I'm learning a handicraft, and although I'll certainly not grow rich by it, at least I'll earn the 100 francs a month necessary to support myself once I'm surer of myself as a draughtsman and find steady work.'

*To Theo van Gogh*
*Saturday, 2 April 1881*
*Brussels*

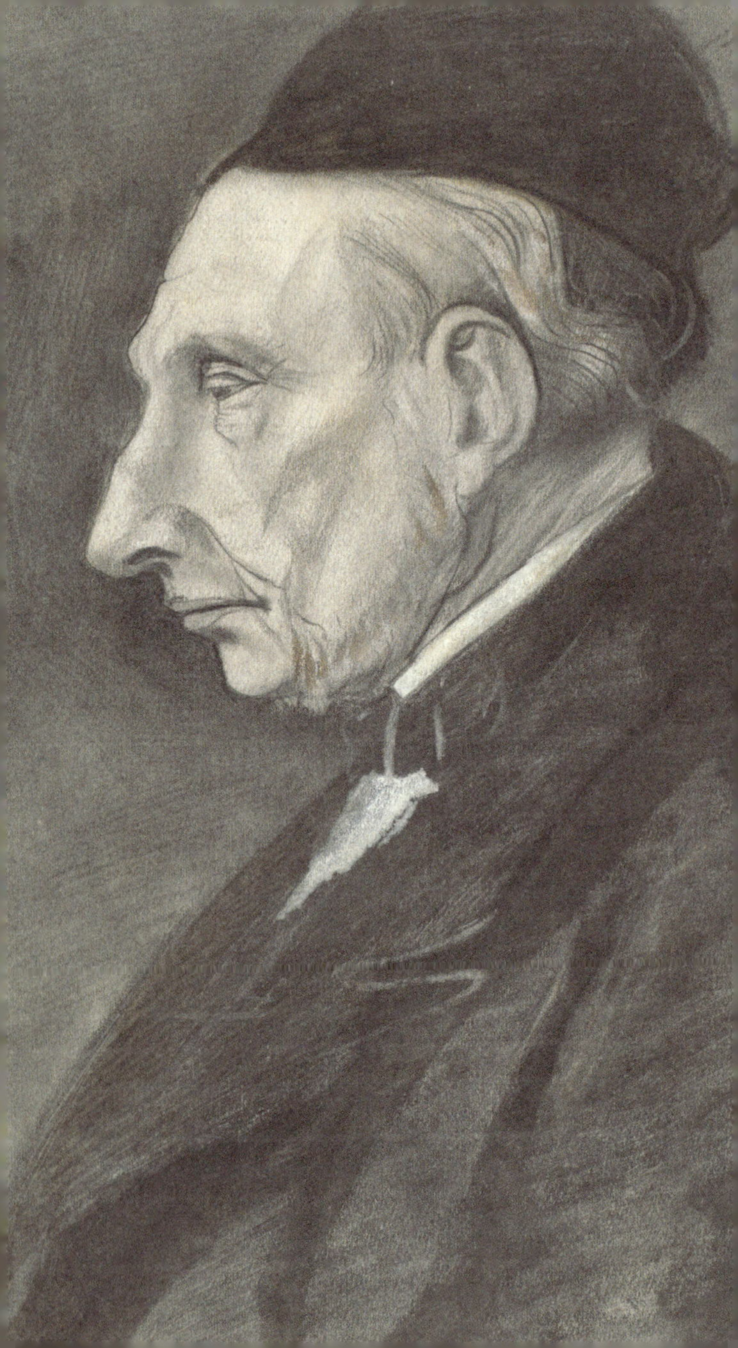

'In short, I dare not cherish any illusions and do fear that Pa and Ma will never take any real pleasure in it. This is hardly surprising and it's not their fault – they haven't learned to see as you and I have learned. They look at different things from us, and we don't see the same things with the same eyes; they don't evoke the same thoughts.

'To wish that it could be different is permissible, to expect it is in my view unwise.'

*To Theo van Gogh*
*Saturday, 26 August 1882*
*The Hague*

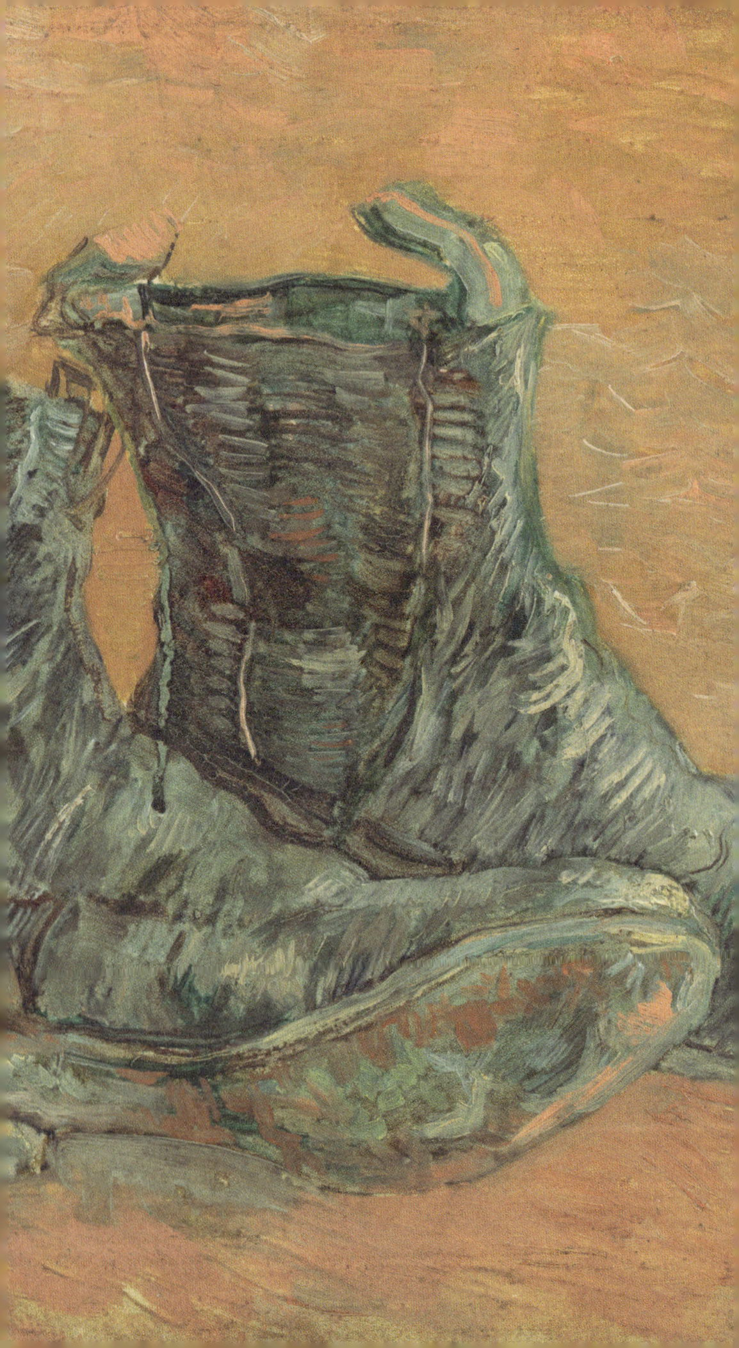

'Naturally I hope that in no way will your help and sympathy come to an end, and that we'll continue to hold out a brotherly hand to each other despite things "the world" opposes.'

*To Theo van Gogh*
*Friday, 12 or Saturday, 13 May 1882*
*The Hague*

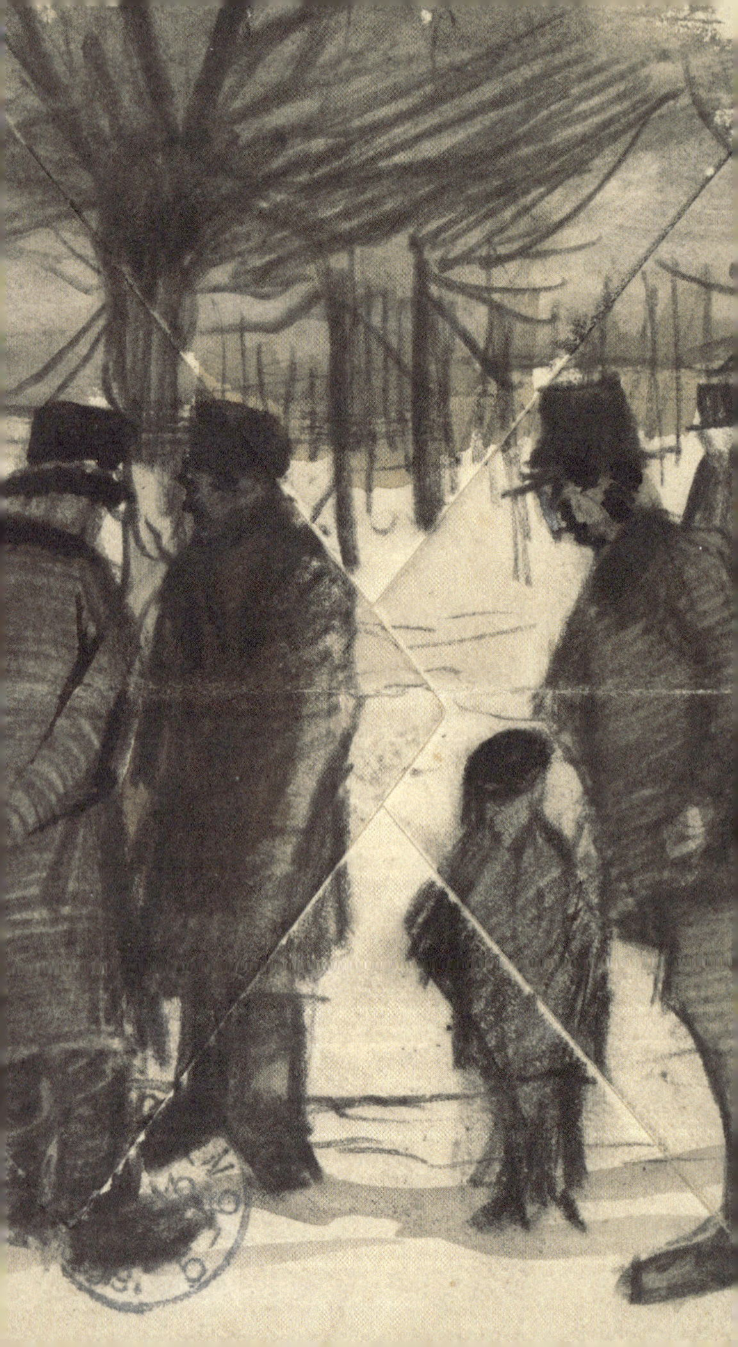

'We know each other so well, his work was my work, the people he knows there I know too, his life was my life, and it was given to me to see so deeply into their family affairs, I think, because I believe that I love them, not so much because I know the particulars of those affairs, but because I feel the tone and feeling of their being and life.'

*To Theo van Gogh*
*Friday, 18 August 1876*
*Isleworth*

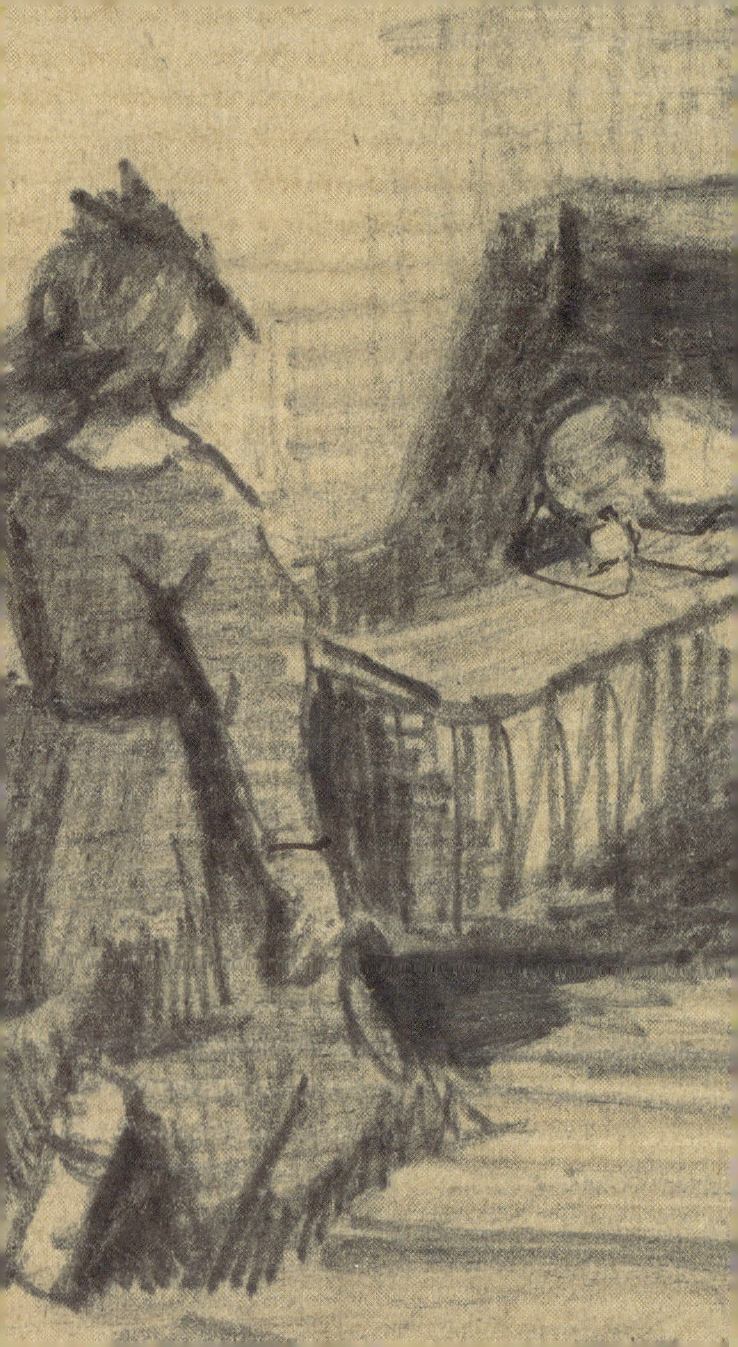

'… next to it a small iron cradle with a green coverlet. I can't look at the last piece of furniture without emotion, for it's a strong and powerful emotion that grips a person when one has sat beside the woman one loves with a child in the cradle near her. …

'You see, I don't know whether you know that feeling, when you're alone at certain moments, that causes one to feel a kind of sigh or lament rising up from within: My God, where is my woman, my God, where is my child – is being alone living?'

*To Theo van Gogh*
*Thursday, 6 and Friday, 7 July 1882*
*The Hague*

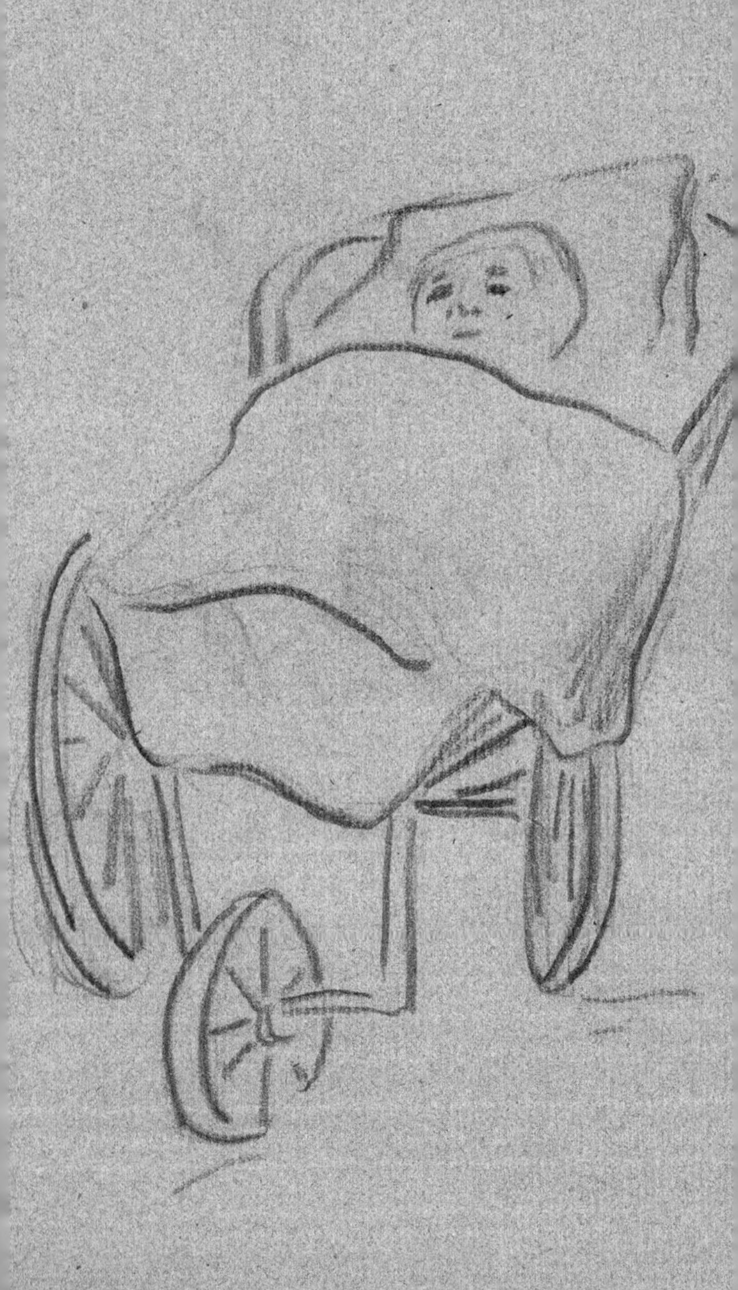

'It touches me so much that you write to me so calmly and so much master of yourself on one of your difficult nights. How I long to hear that you've come through safely and that your child lives. How happy Theo will be, and a new sun will rise in him when he sees you recovering. Forgive me if I tell you that to my mind recovery takes a long time and is no easier than being ill. Our parents knew *that* too, and following them in that is, I believe, what one calls duty. Well for my part, I'm thinking about all of you these days.'

*To Jo van Gogh-Bonger*
*Friday, 31 January 1890*
*Saint-Rémy-de-Provence*

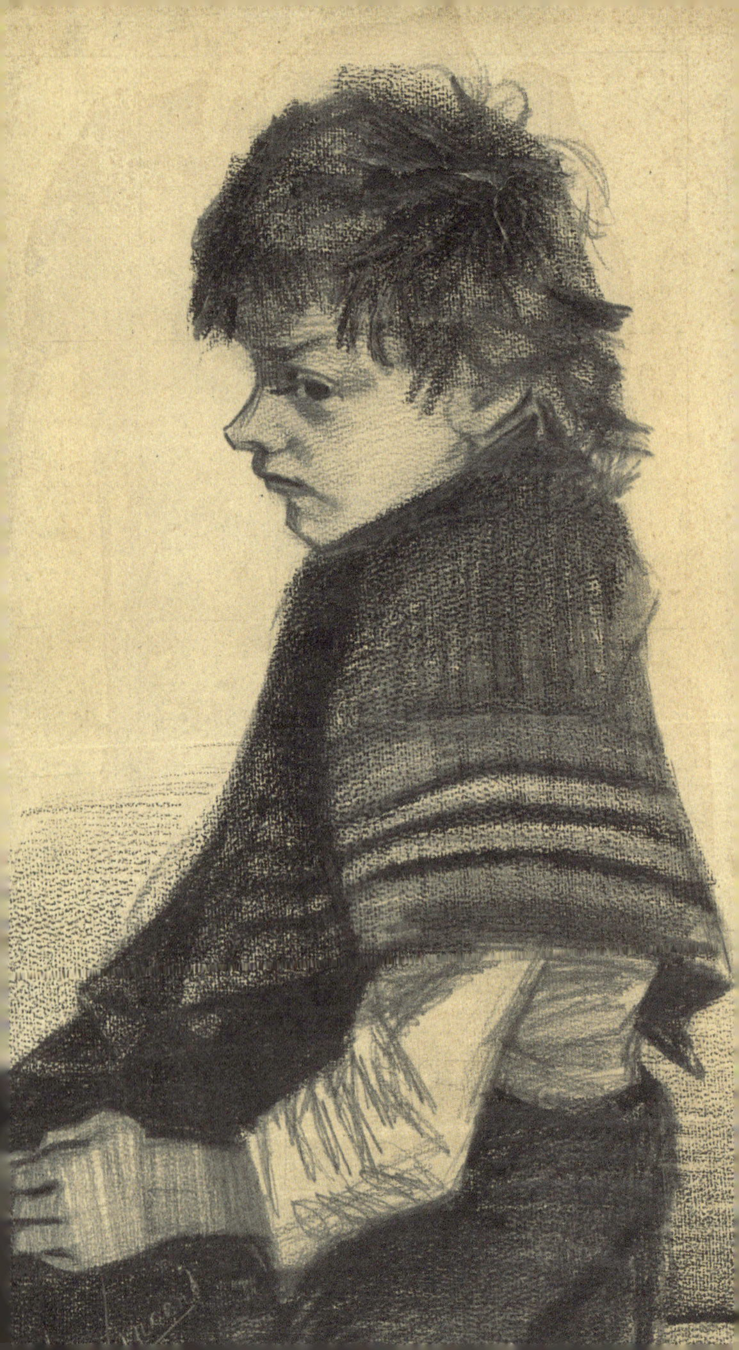

'Once you've attained a position and can maintain a certain status, then you'll find wife and children and domestic happiness. This is a fine promise that society makes, but does it also keep that promise?

'Society leaves *everyone* and all ways of doing things relatively disappointed. I say this in all mildness and not as a reproach, not *in the least or slightest* as such.

'I often think that there's good in every energetic movement.'

*To Theo van Gogh*
*on or about Sunday, 21 September 1884*
*Nuenen*

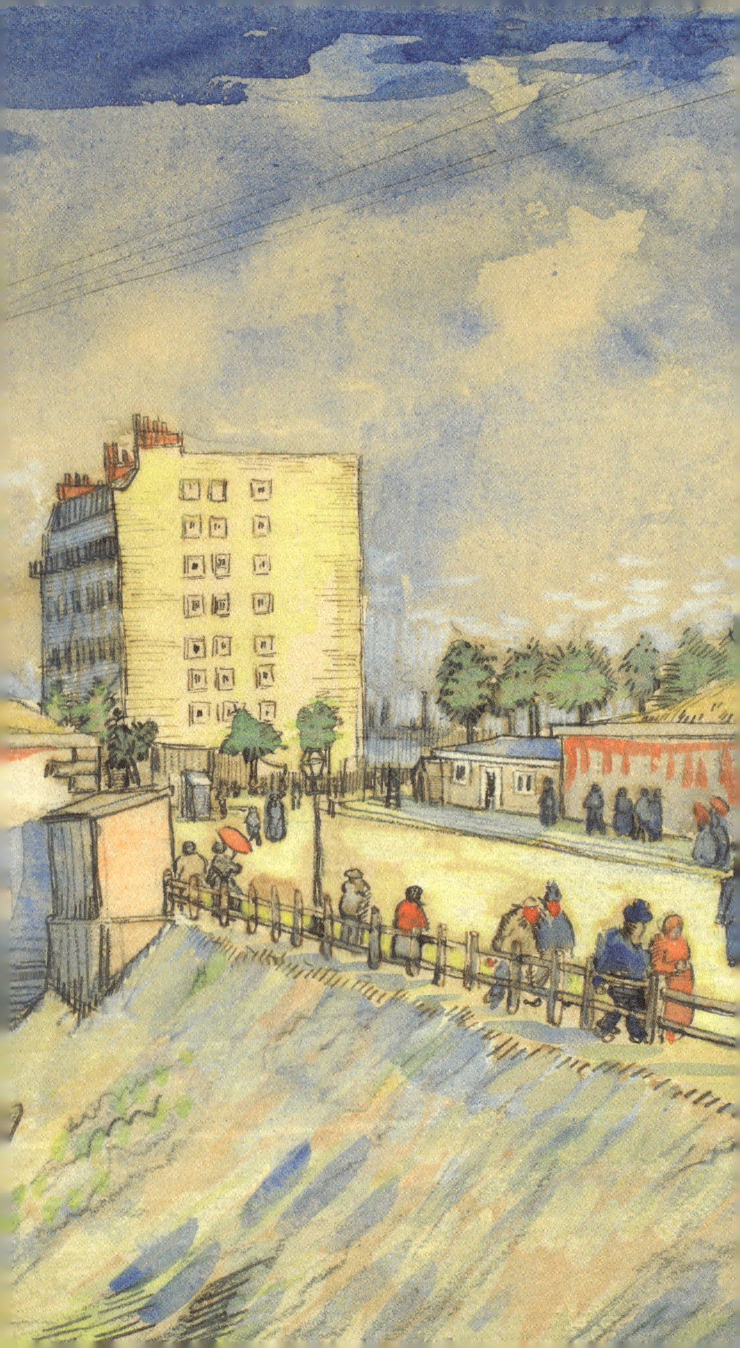

'All these things, family, native country, are
perhaps more appealing in the imagination
of such as us – who do fairly well without a
native country, as well as a family – than in
any reality. It always seems to me that I'm
a traveller who's going somewhere and to
a destination.'

*To Theo van Gogh*
*Monday, 6 August 1888*
*Arles*

# HOPE

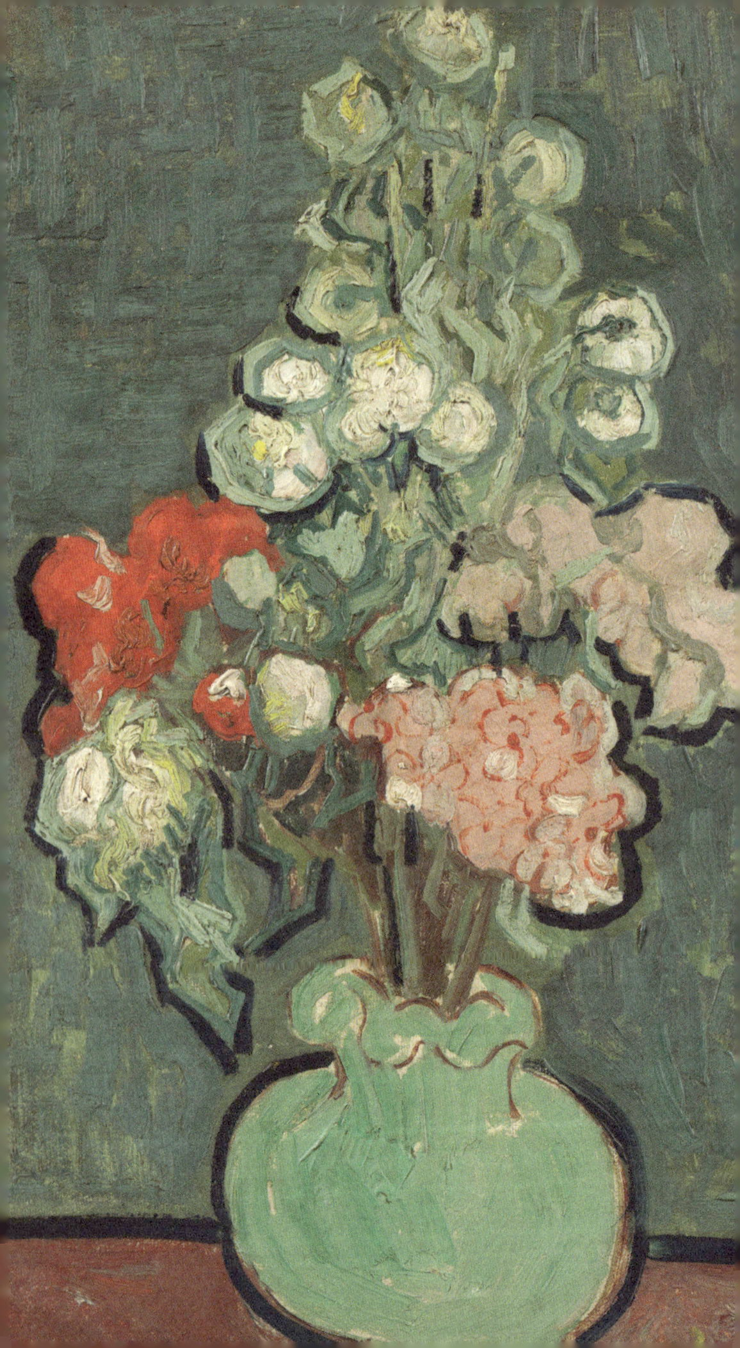

'You can see, then, that I'm working like mad, but for the moment it isn't giving very heartening results. But I have hopes that these thorns will bear white flowers in their time, and that this apparently sterile struggle is nothing other than a labour of giving birth. First pain, then joy afterwards.'

*To Theo van Gogh*
*Friday, 24 September 1880*
*Cuesmes*

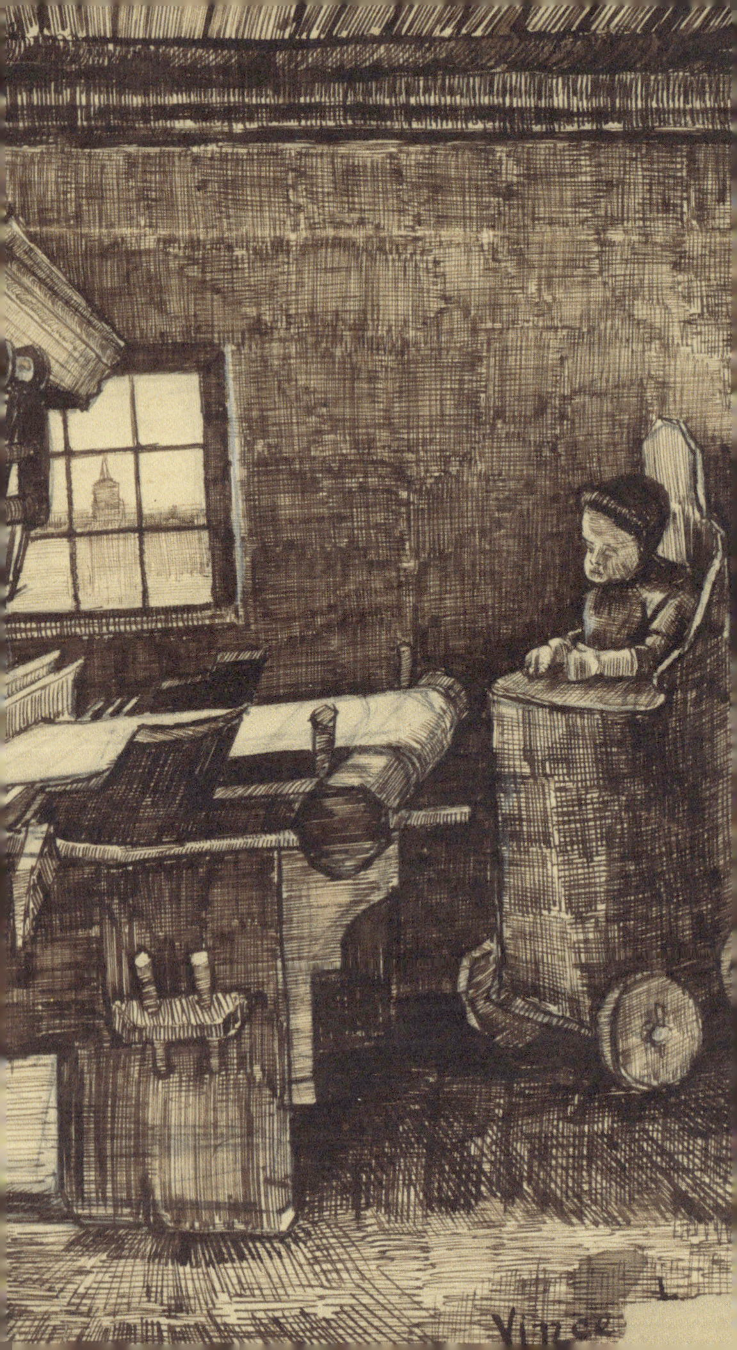

Vince

'At present, dimly on the horizon, here it comes to me nevertheless – hope – that intermittent hope that has sometimes consoled me in my lonely life.

'Now I'd like to see you taking a very large share in this belief that we'll be relatively successful in founding something lasting.'

*To Paul Gauguin*
*Wednesday, 3 October 1888*
*Arles*

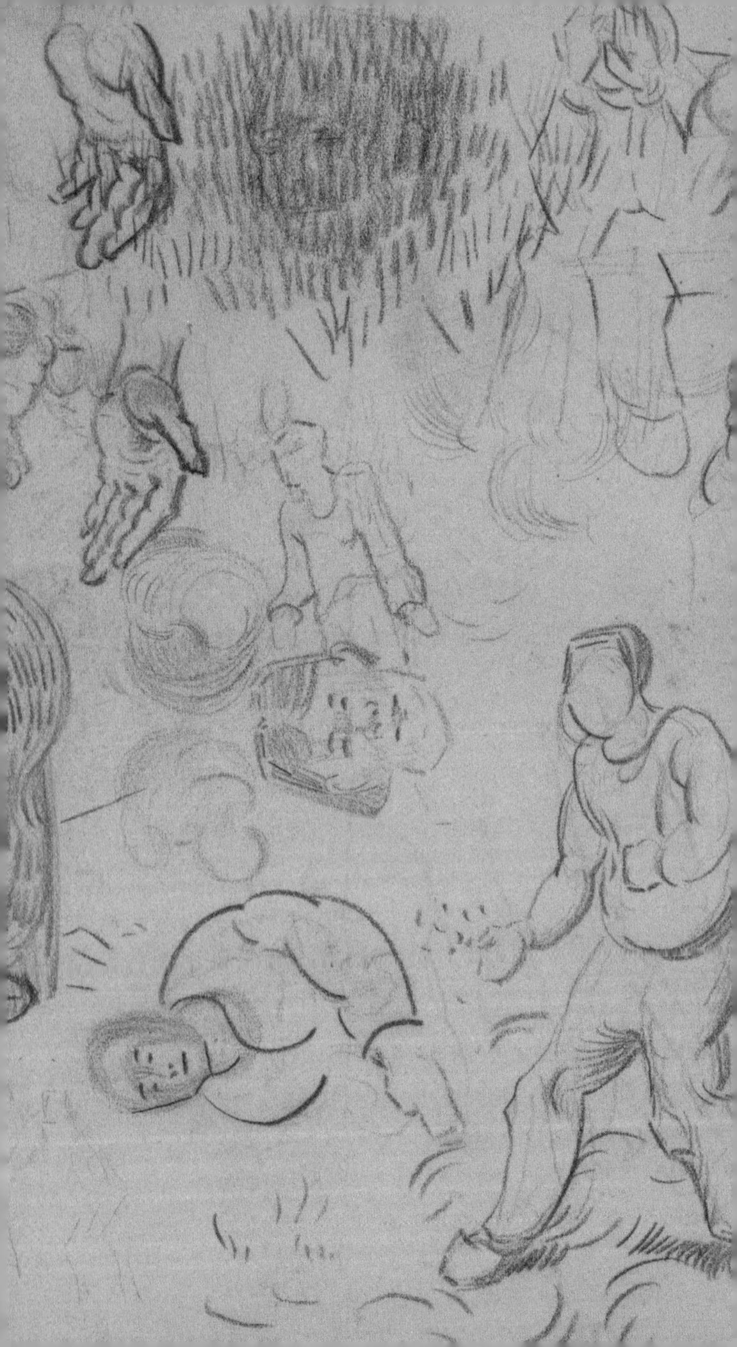

'It's not pleasant to do sketches like the enclosed and then be unable to finish them. I hate this so much myself that I do them very rarely, purely to see whether I've found this or that and how far I've got. But I have hope and interest again now precisely because I have a large number of studies behind me.'

*To Theo van Gogh*
*on or about Friday, 2 March 1883*
*The Hague*

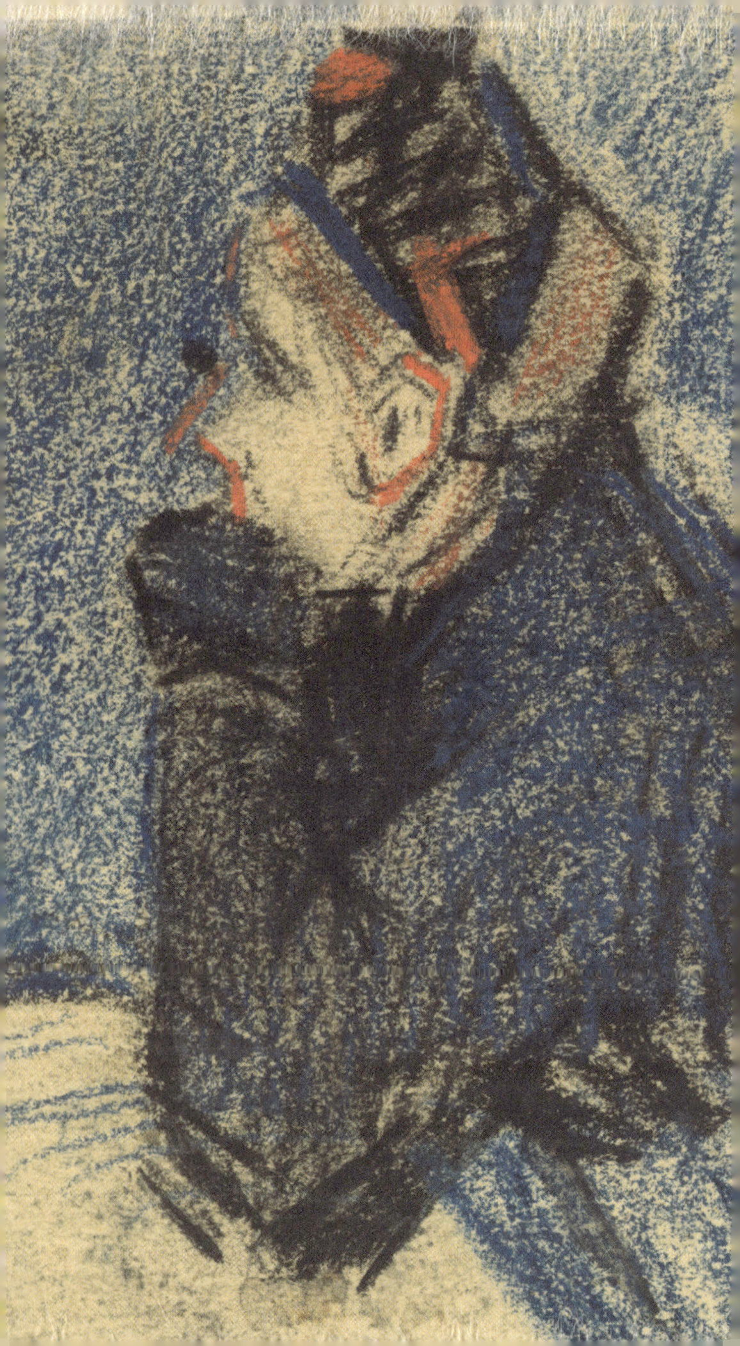

'The joy of others may embitter jealous hearts, but it fortifies submissive hearts; it is the ray of sunshine that opens up those two lovely flowers called "confidence" and "hope".'

*To Theo van Gogh*
*Saturday, 7 and Sunday, 8 October 1876*
*Isleworth*

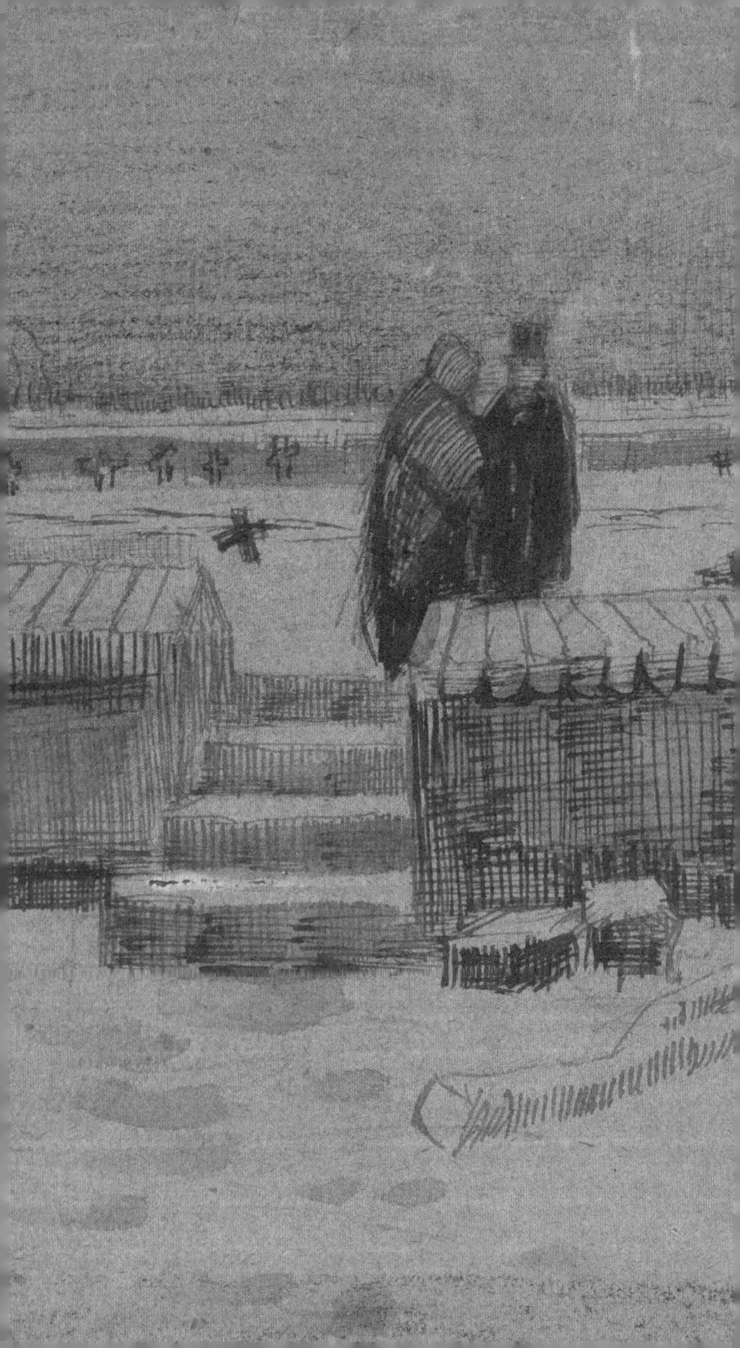

'To many it would no doubt appear foolish and superstitious to believe in any improvement for the better. Sometimes in winter it's so bitterly cold that one says, it's simply too cold, what do I care whether summer comes, the bad outweighs the good. But whether we like it or not, an end finally comes to the hard frost, and one fine morning the wind has turned and we have a thaw.'

*To Theo van Gogh*
*between about Monday, 11*
*and Thursday, 14 August 1879*
*Cuesmes*

# HARMONY

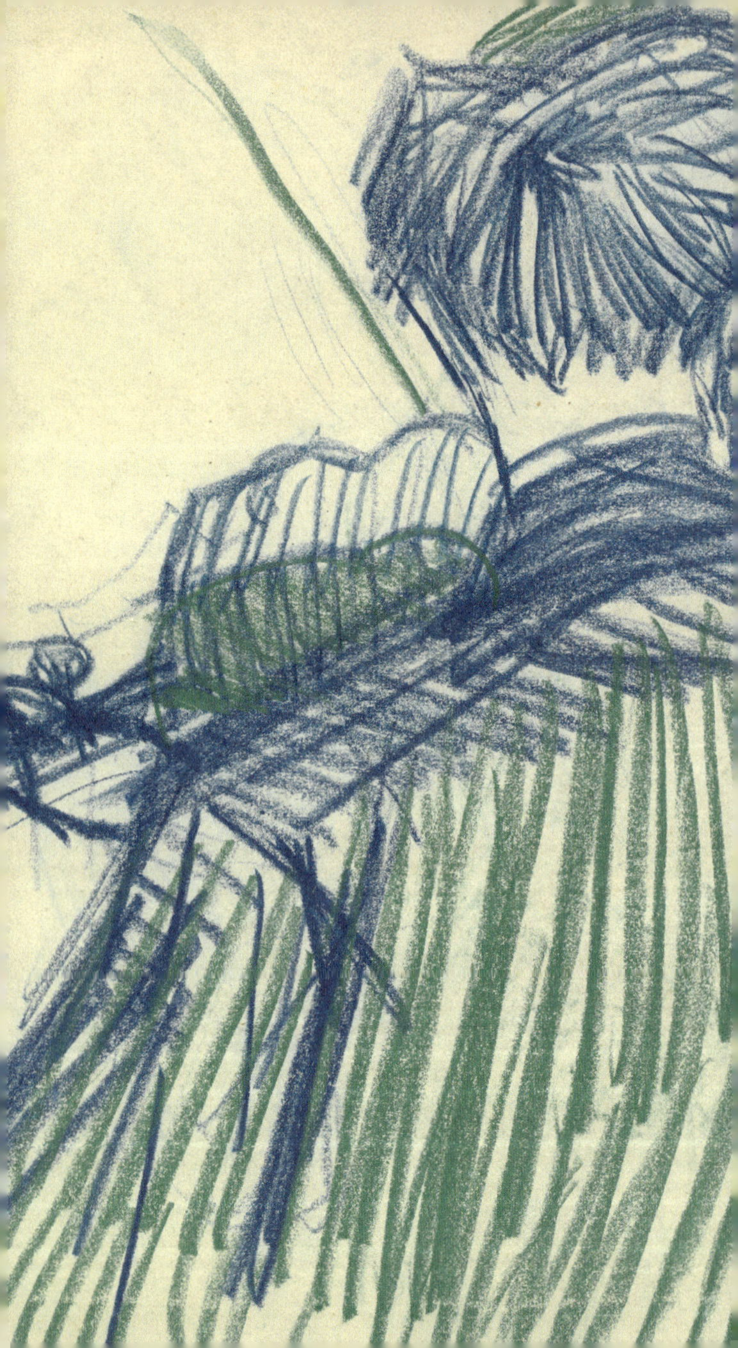

'Even though I'm often in a mess, inside me there's still a calm, pure harmony and music. In the poorest little house, in the filthiest corner, I see paintings or drawings. And my mind turns in that direction as if with an irresistible urge.'

*To Theo van Gogh*
*on or about Friday, 21 July 1882*
*The Hague*

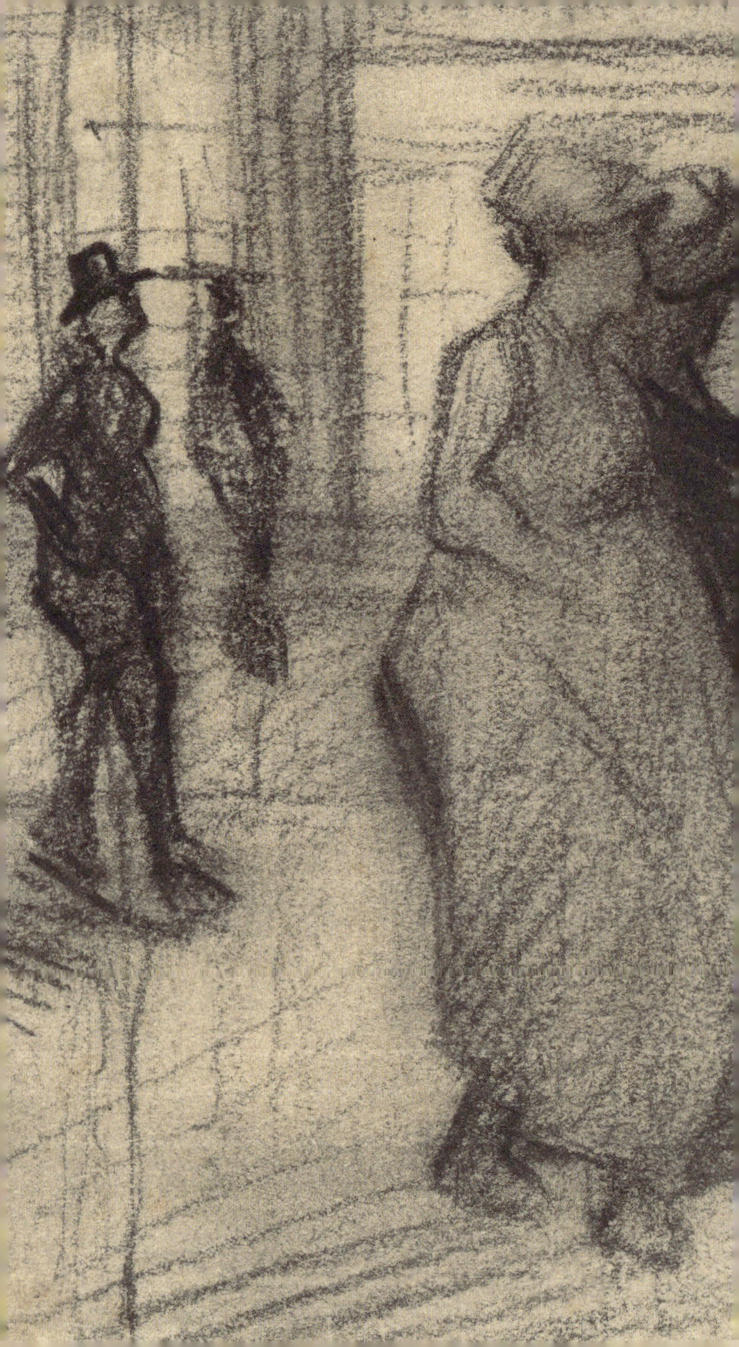

'With a permanent relationship one finds great inner calm and is in harmony with nature in my view ... And so, in my view, he who orders his life in harmony with the eternal laws of nature and of morality contributes to reform and progress, and consequently to the restoration of things that are disorientated in contemporary society.'

*To Theo van Gogh*
*Sunday, 3 June 1883*
*The Hague*

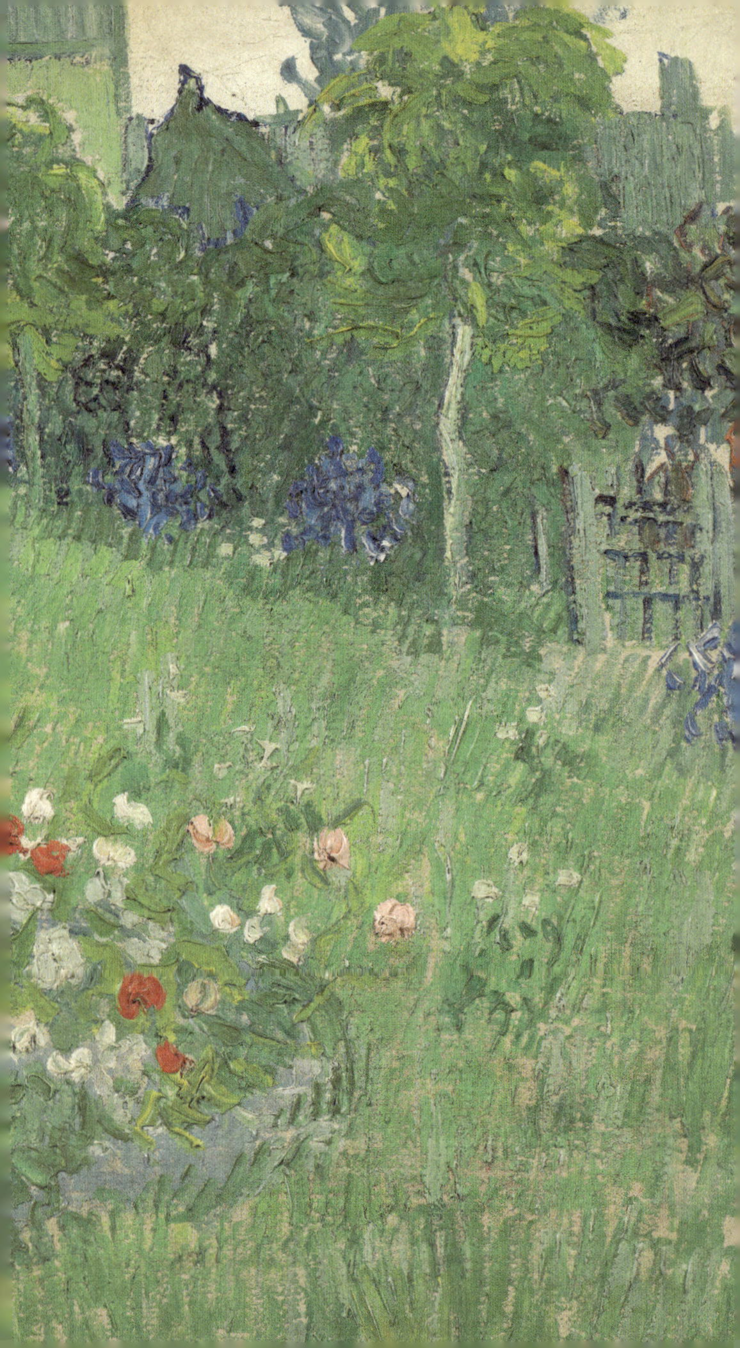

'When she's past her old misery, there will be a completely new period in her life: she won't get back her spring – that is over, and was cruel anyway – but her *second growth* can be all the fresher. You know how, in the middle of summer when the greatest heat has passed, the trees throw out fresh young shoots, a new layer of young green over the old, faded one.'

*To Theo van Gogh*
*Sunday, 2 July 1882*
*The Hague*

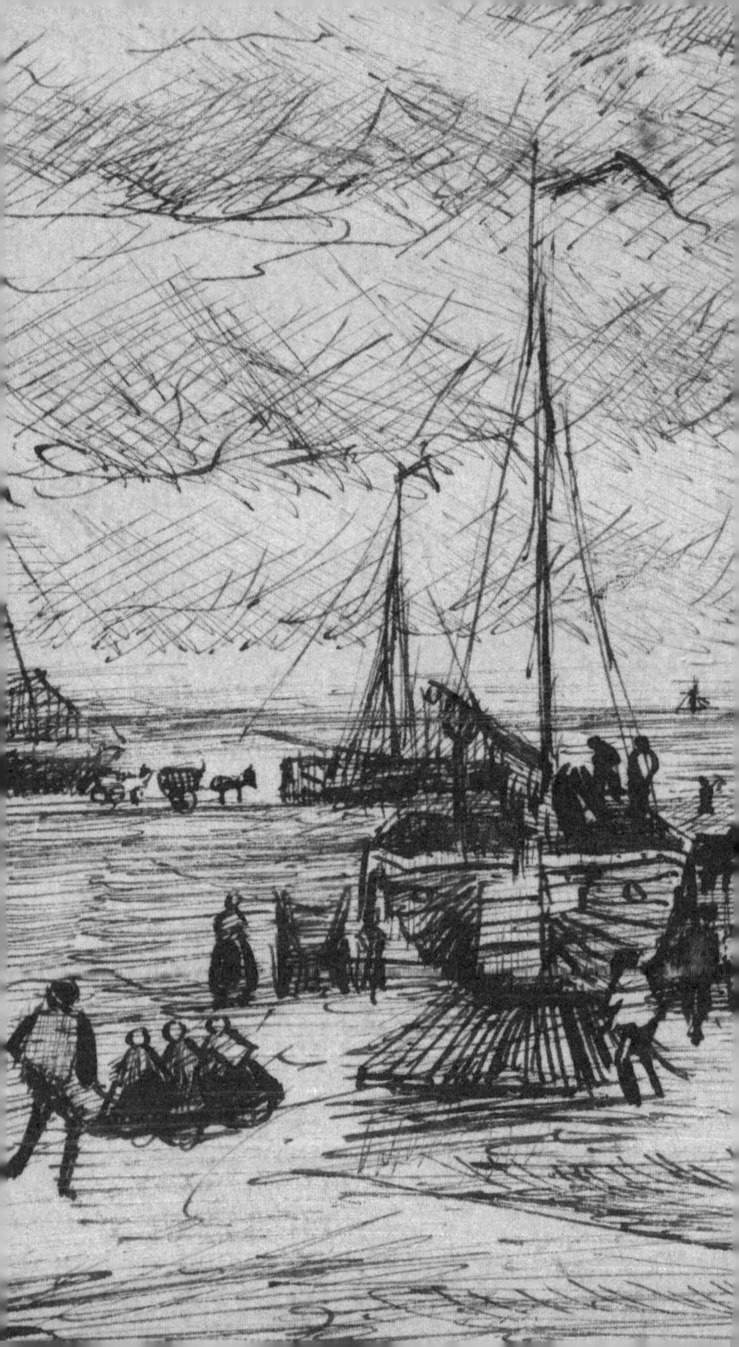

'You're now beginning to enter waters that are throwing you off balance, inasmuch as the rapport with nature seems to be broken. Take that very coolly as a sign of aberration; say, oh no, not that way if you please.'

*To Theo van Gogh*
*Friday, 12 October 1883*
*Hoogeveen*

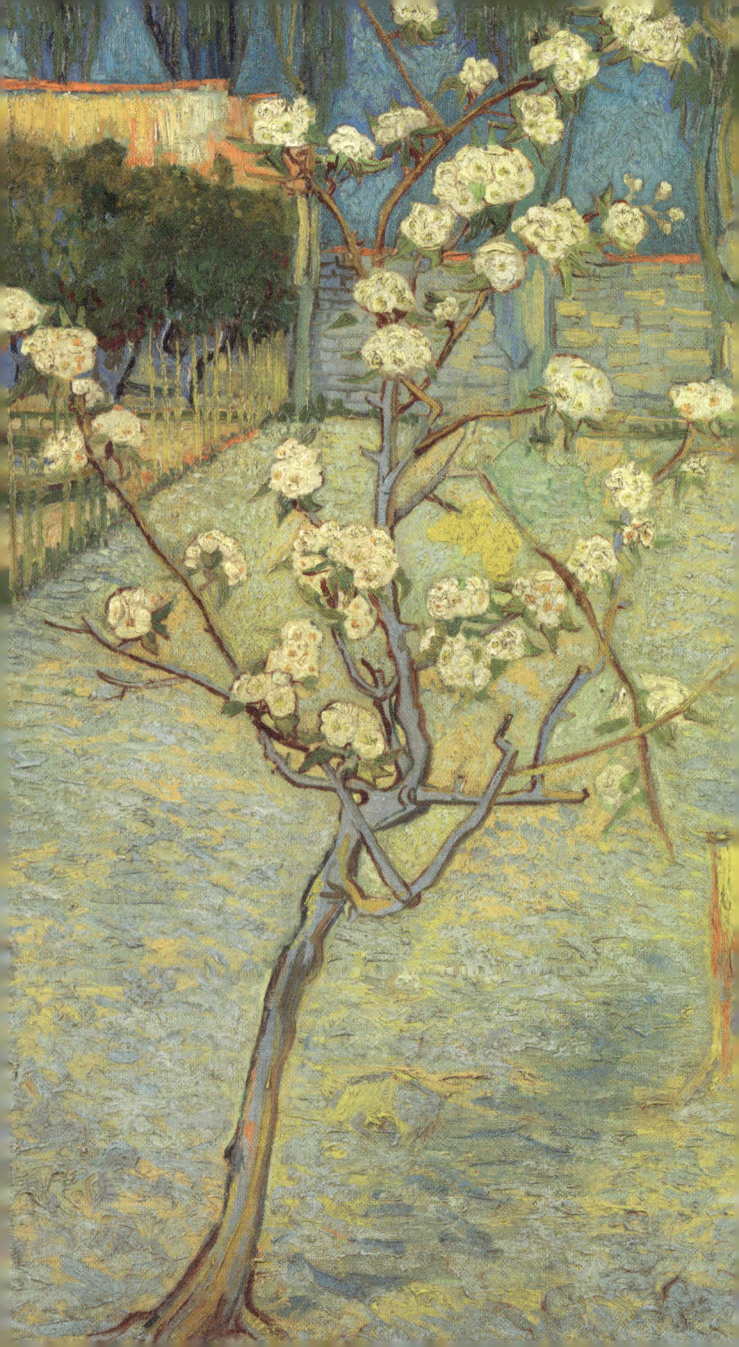

'For a long time I've been touched by the
fact that Japanese artists very often made
exchanges among themselves. It clearly
proves that they liked one another and
stuck together, and that there was a certain
harmony among them and that they did
indeed live a kind of brotherly life, in
a natural way and not in the midst
of intrigues.'

*To Emile Bernard*
*Wednesday, 3 October 1888*
*Arles*

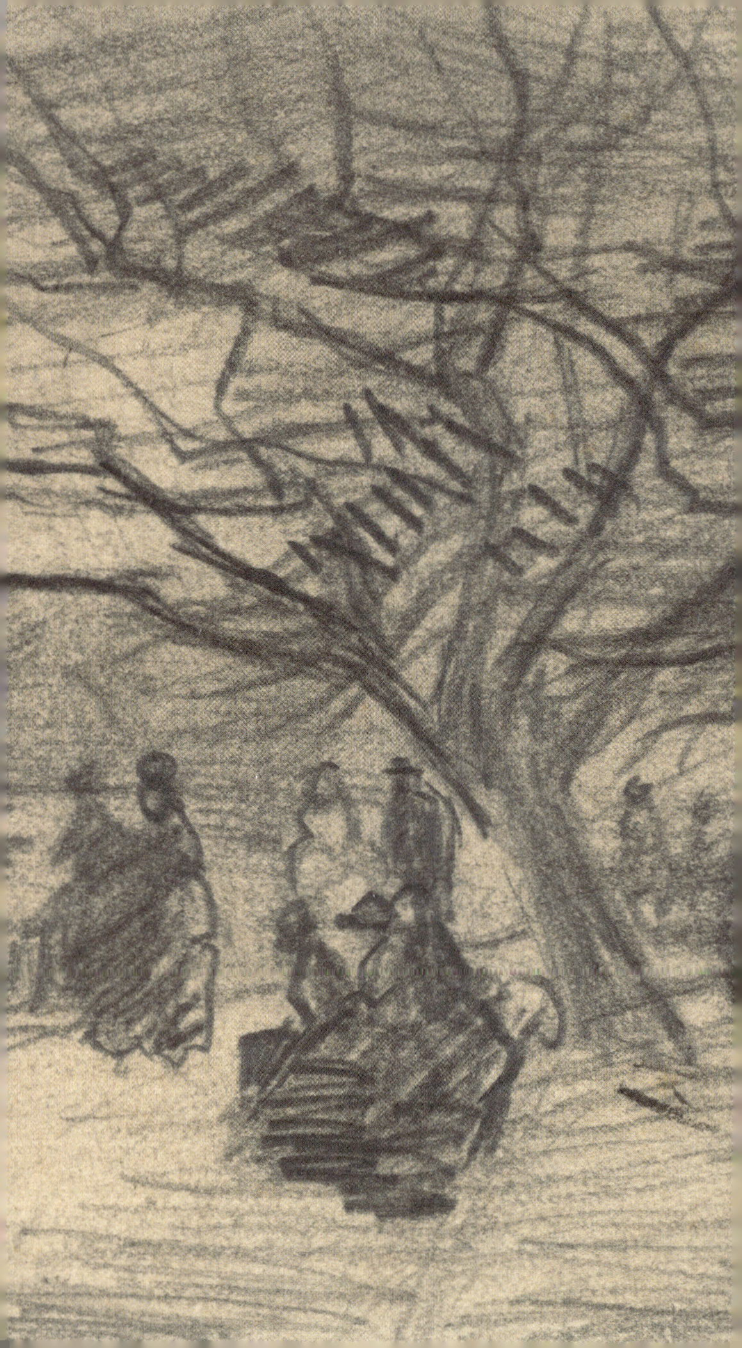

'The fact remains that provided we lived in harmony and with an understanding not to quarrel, we'd gain a firmer position as far as reputation goes.

'Each of us living alone, we live like madmen or criminals, in appearance at least, and to some extent in reality, too.'

*To Theo van Gogh*
*Thursday, 9 August 1888*
*Arles*

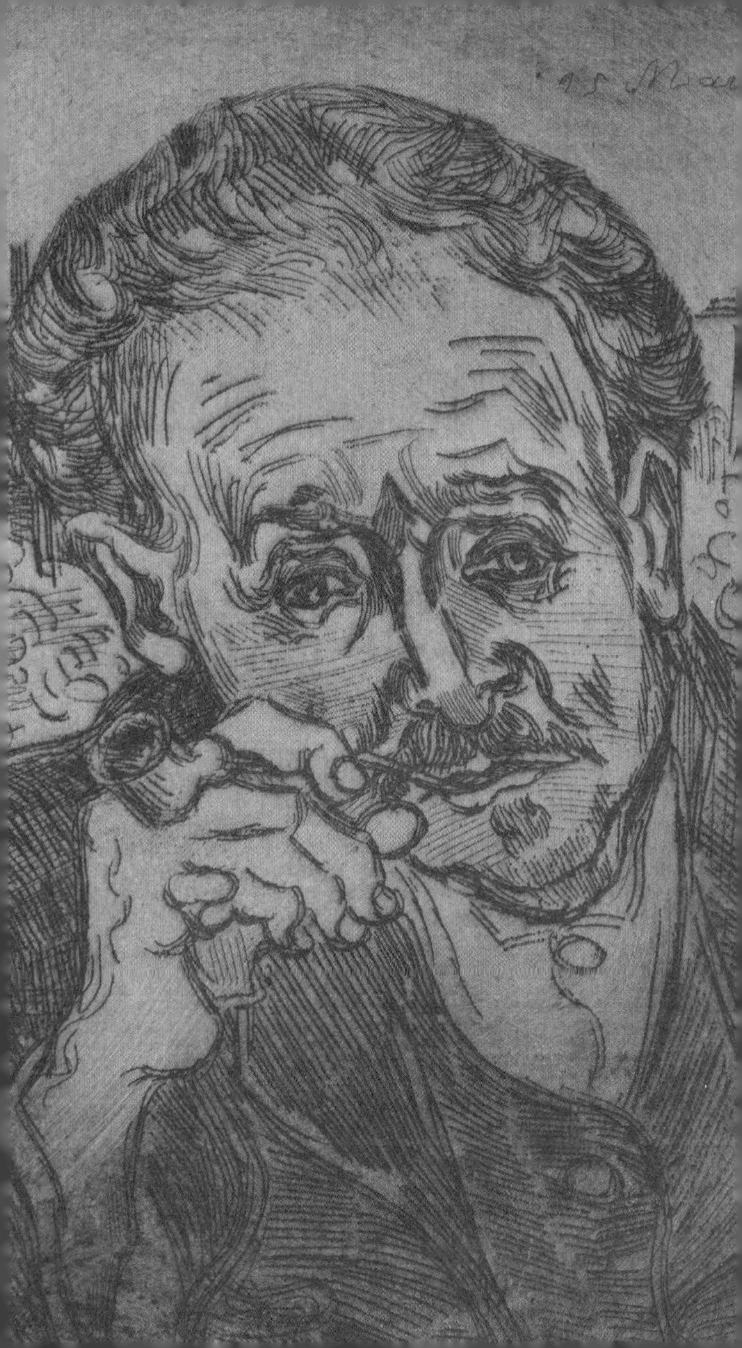

'I very much like to believe that illnesses sometimes cure us, i.e. that when the illness comes to a crisis it's a thing necessary to the recovery of a normal state of body.'

*To Theo van Gogh and Jo van Gogh-Bonger*
*Saturday, 6 July 1889*
*Saint-Rémy-de-Provence*

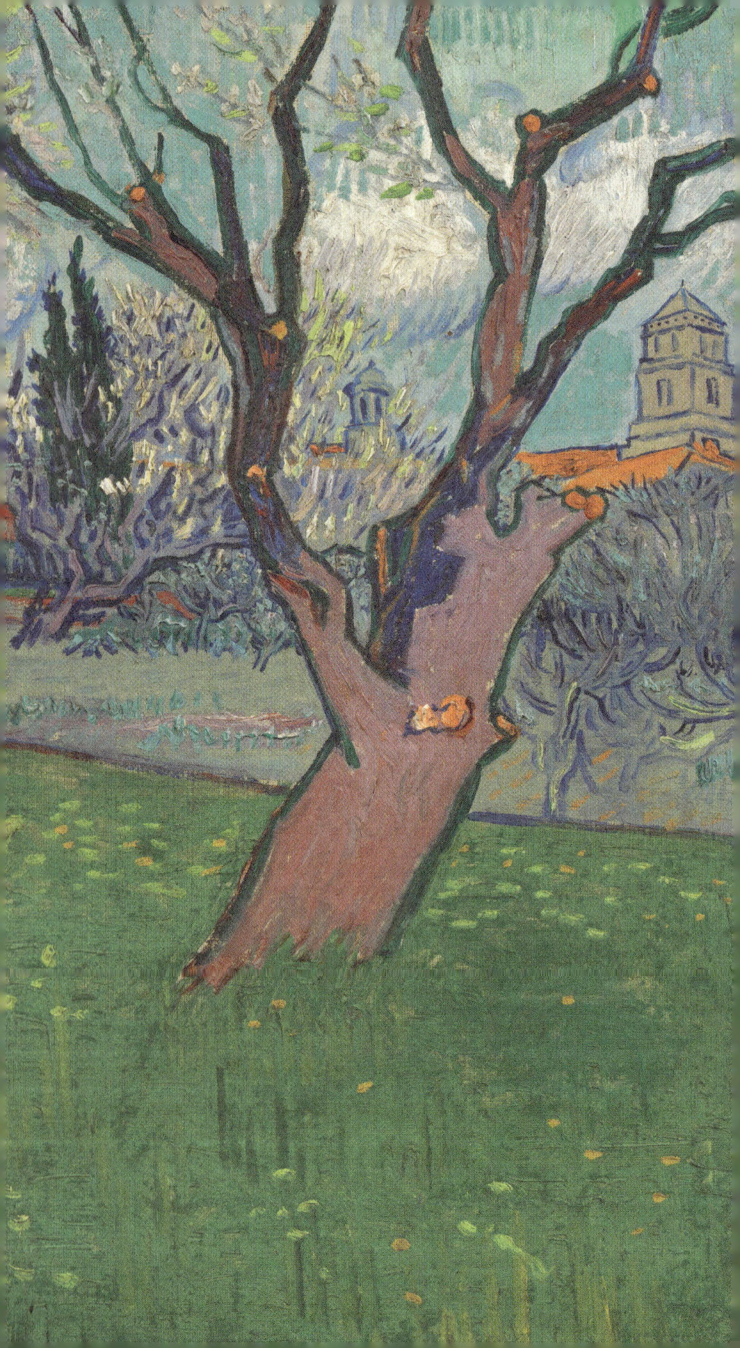

'I always have an animal's coarse appetites. I forget everything for the external beauty of things, *which I'm unable to render* because I make it ugly in my painting, and coarse, whereas nature seems perfect to me.

'Now, however, the energy of my bony carcass is such that it goes straight to the target; from that comes a perhaps sometimes original sincerity in what I make, if, that is, the subject lends itself to my rough and unskilful execution.'

*To Paul Gauguin*
*Wednesday, 3 October 1888*
*Arles*

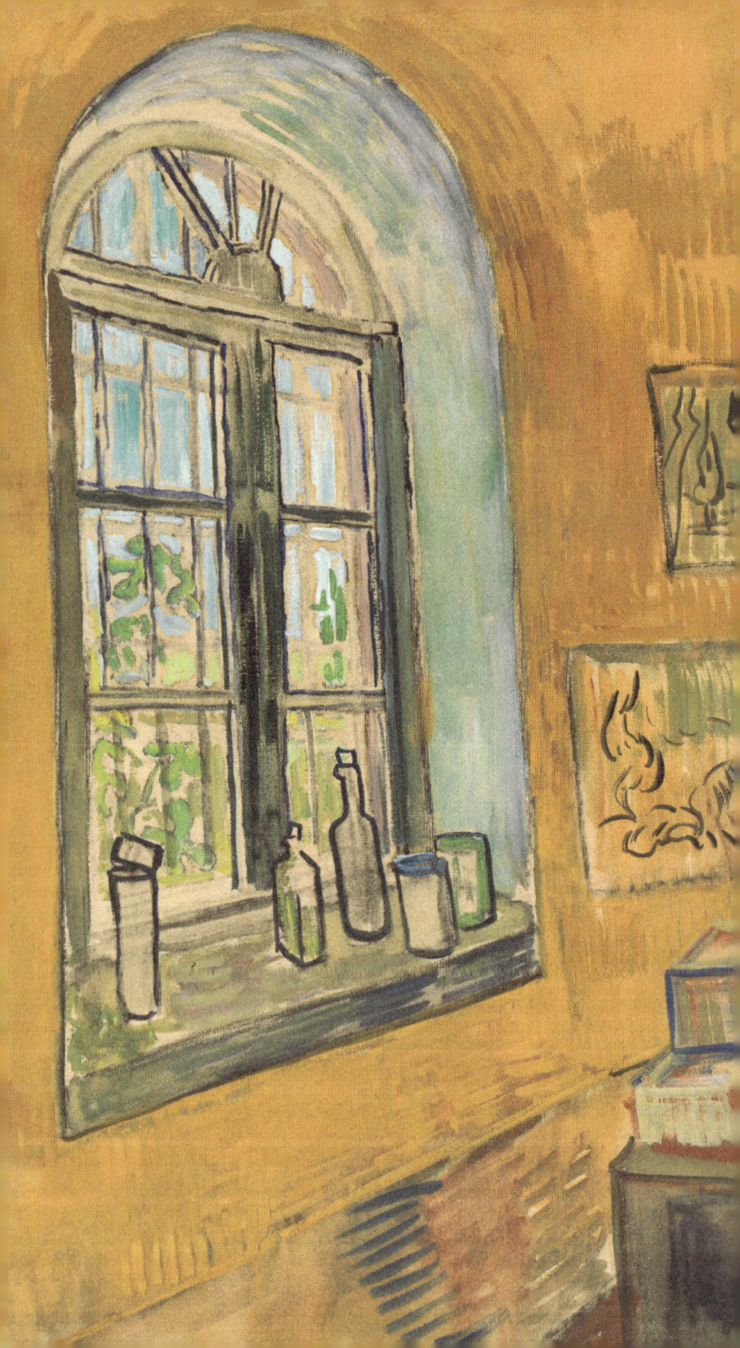

'This morning I saw the countryside from my window a long time before sunrise with nothing but the morning star, which looked very big. … with the expression of all the intimacy and all the great peace and majesty that it has, adding to it a feeling so heartbreaking, so personal. These emotions I do not detest.

'I still have remorse, and enormously when I think of my work, so little in harmony with what I'd have wished to do. I hope that in the long run it will make me do better things, but we aren't there yet.'

*To Theo van Gogh*
*between about Friday, 31 May*
*and about Thursday, 6 June 1889*
*Saint-Rémy-de-Provence*

# MEANING

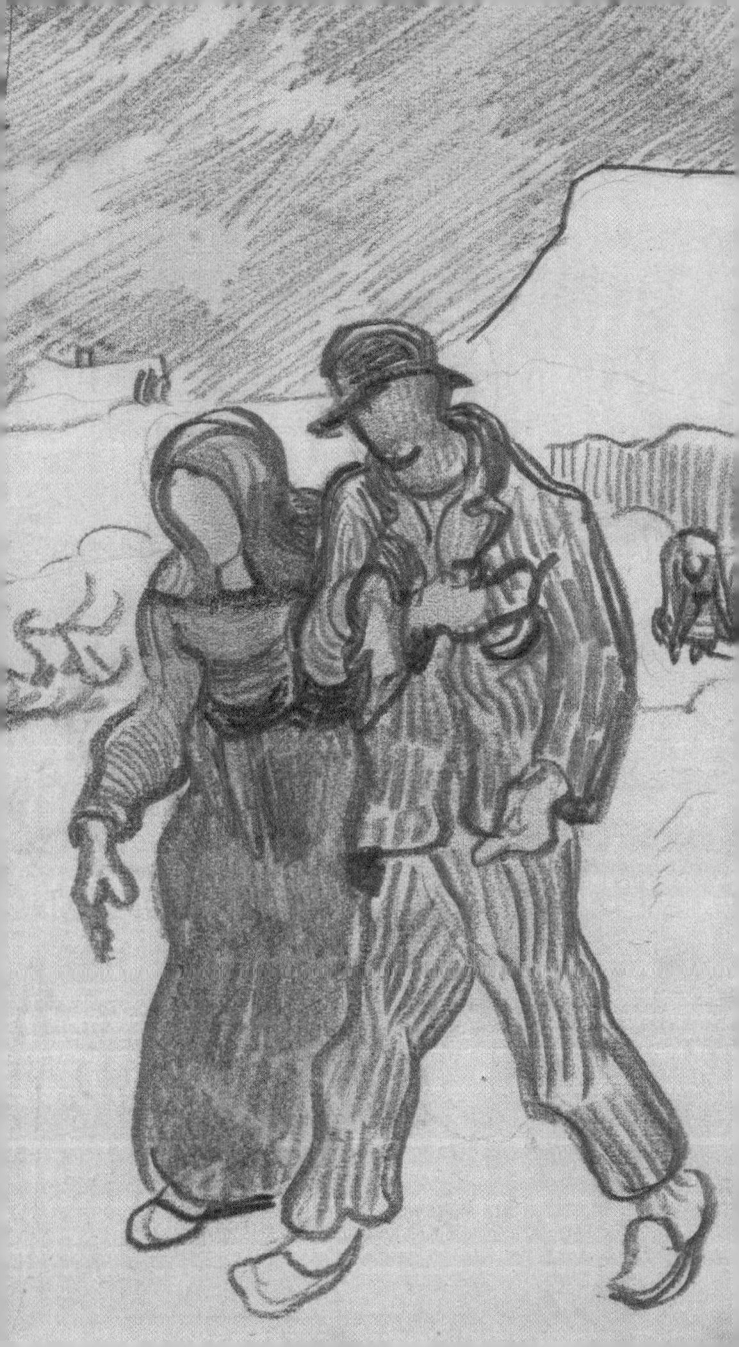

'Now those with an eye for it see something beautiful and good in *all* weathers, find snow beautiful and burning sun beautiful and storm beautiful and calm beautiful, cold good and heat, are fond of all seasons and don't want to miss a single day of the year ...'

*To Theo van Gogh*
*on or about Thursday, 10 May 1883*
*The Hague*



ADVICE FOR
THE SOUL

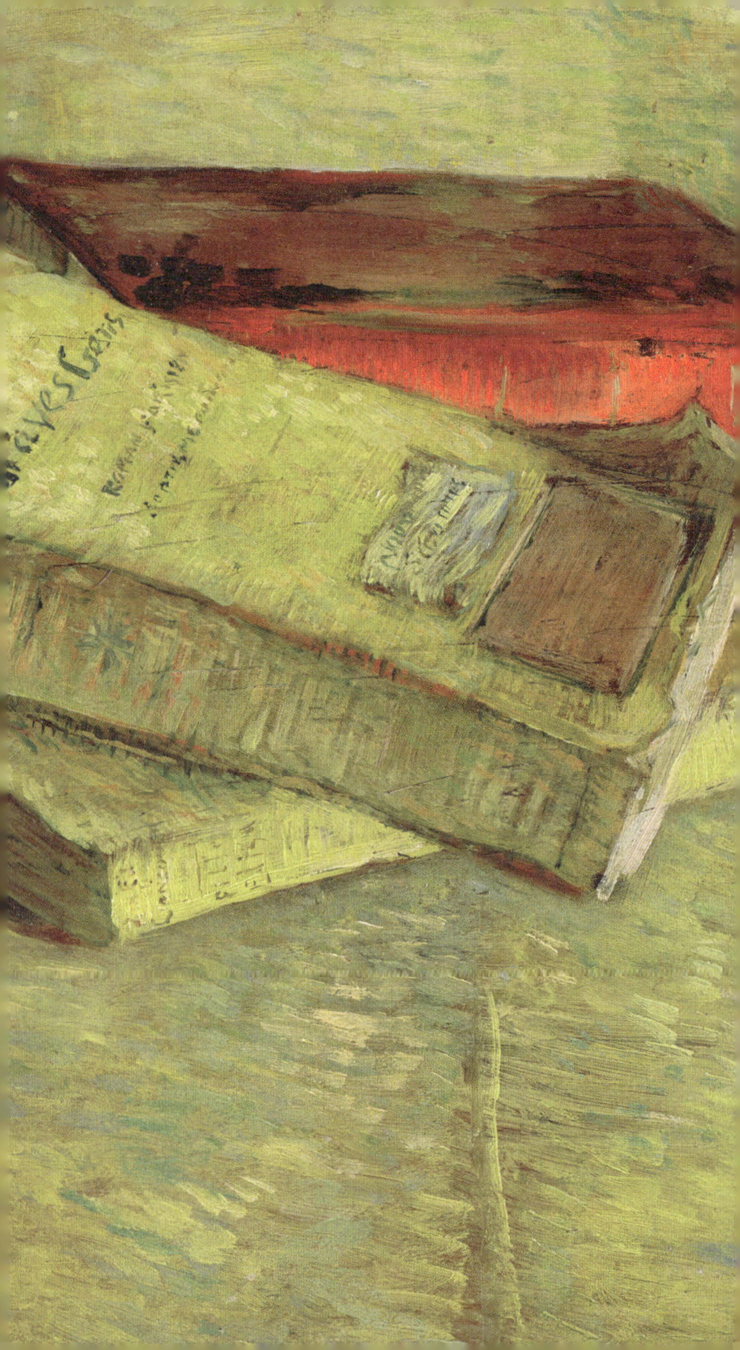

'If one were to say but few words, though ones with meaning, one would do better than to say many that were only empty sounds, and just as easy to utter as they were of little use.'

*To Theo van Gogh*
*Wednesday, 3 April 1878*
*Amsterdam*

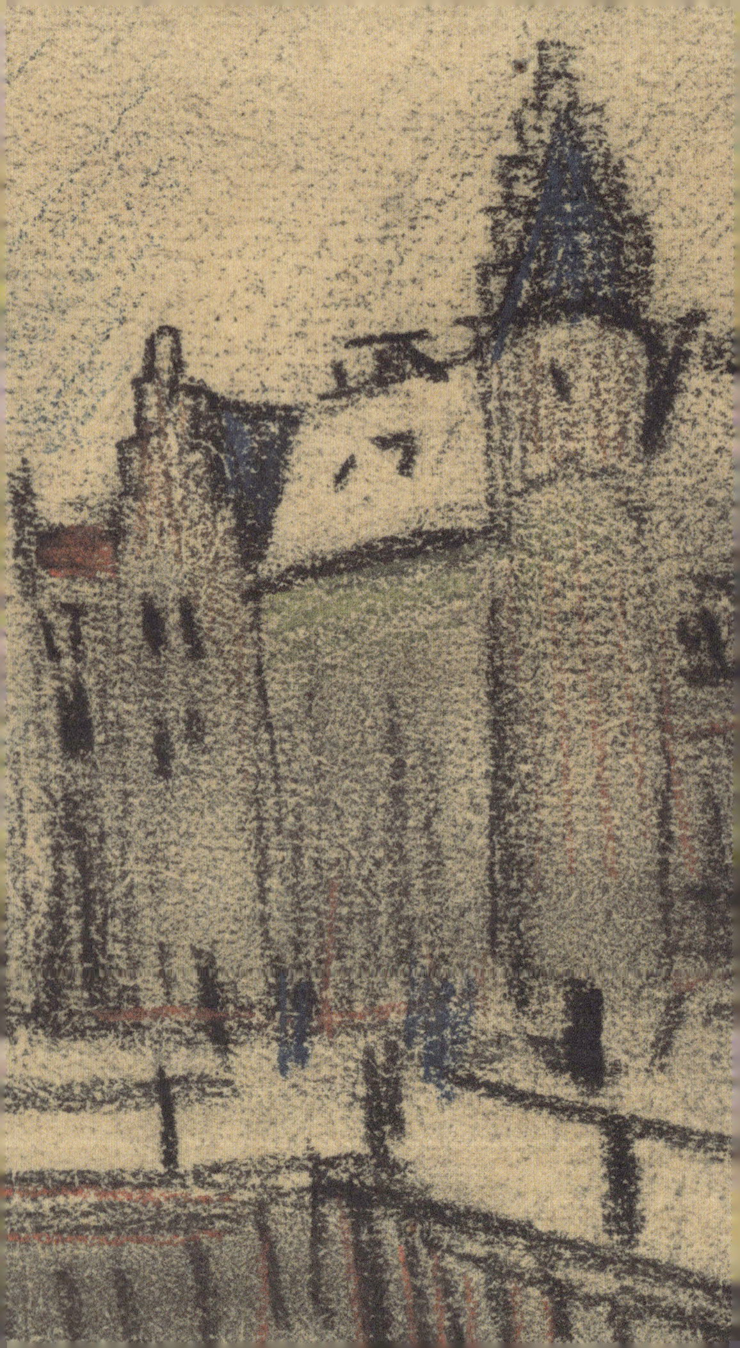

'All your kindnesses for me, I've found them
greater than ever today.

'I can't tell you it as I feel it, but I assure
you that that kindness has been of great
worth, and if you don't see its results,
my dear brother, don't be upset about it,
you will still have your kindness.'

*To Theo van Gogh*
*Sunday, 21 April 1889*
*Arles*

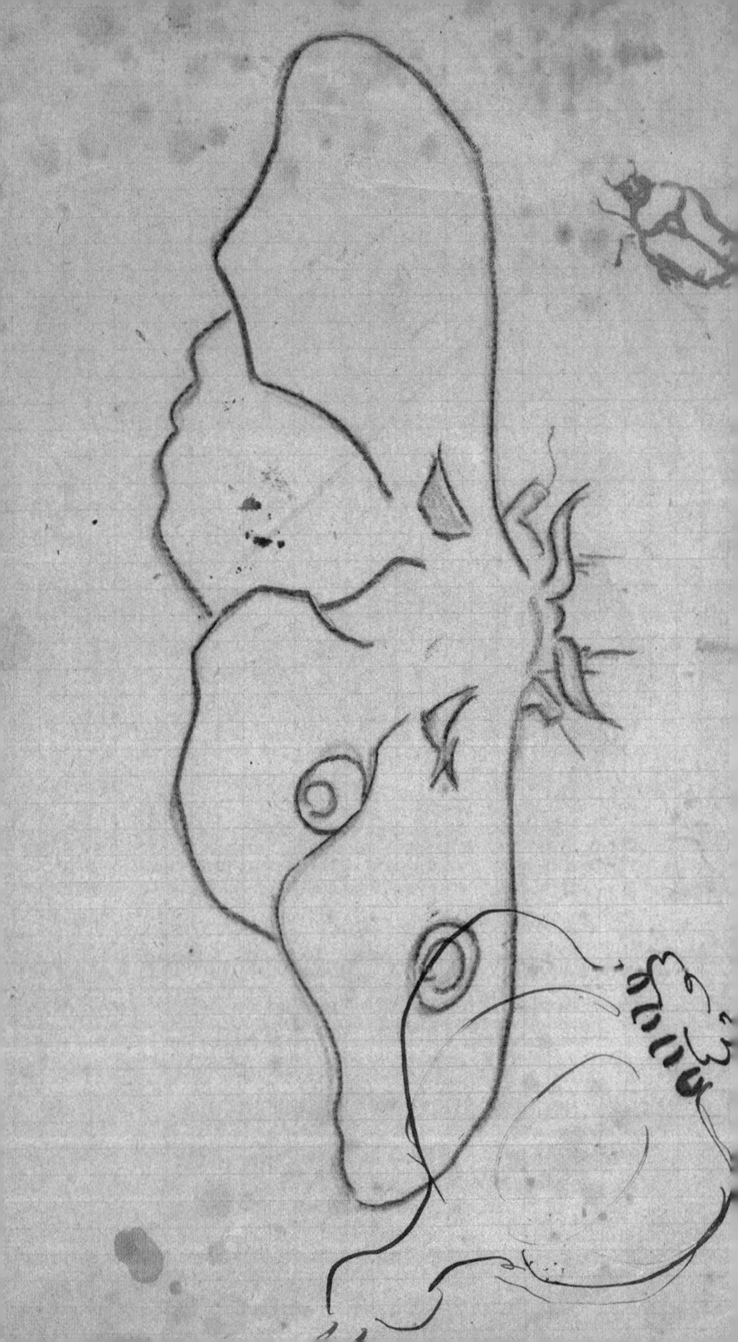

'For the great doesn't happen through impulse alone, and is a succession of little things that are brought together.'

*To Theo van Gogh*
*Sunday, 22 October 1882*
*The Hague*

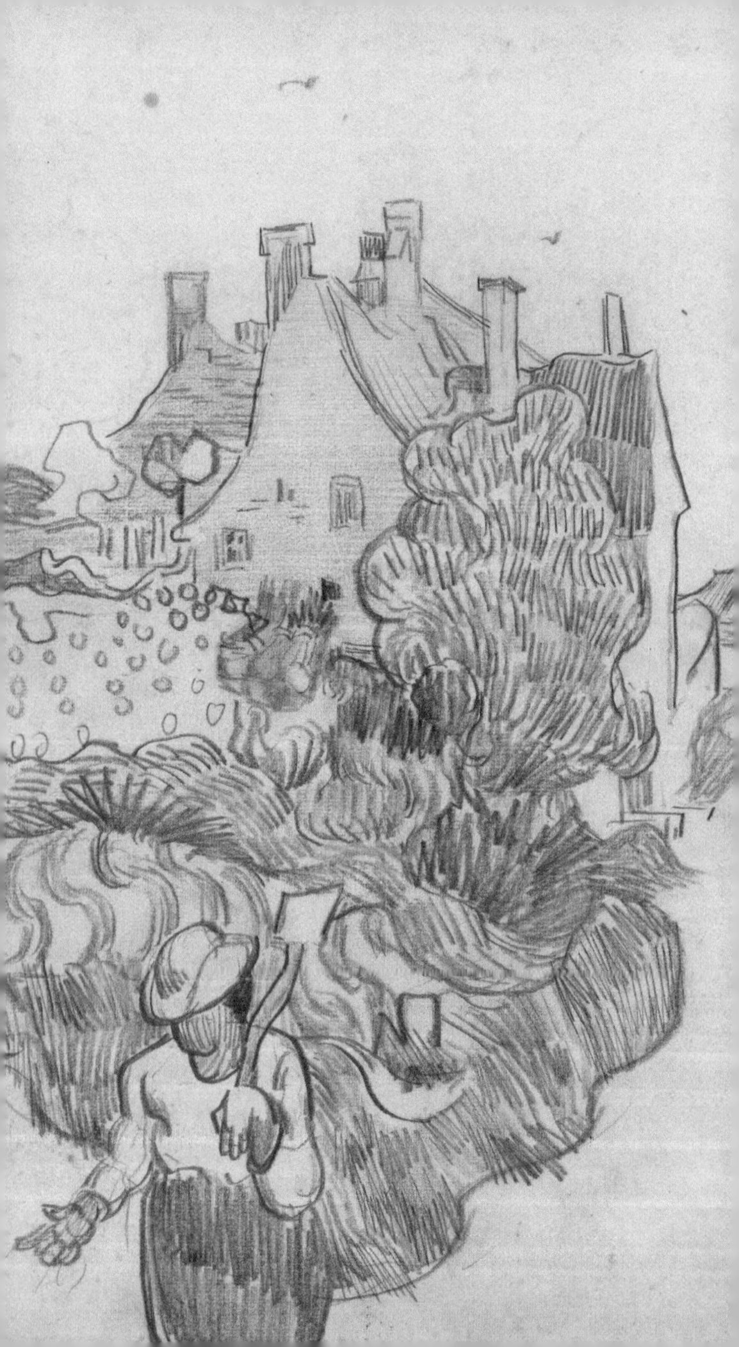

'In my view I'm often *very rich*, not in money, but rich (although not every day exactly) because I've found my work – have something which I live for heart and soul and which gives inspiration and meaning to life.'

*To Theo van Gogh*
*Sunday, 11 March 1883*
*The Hague*

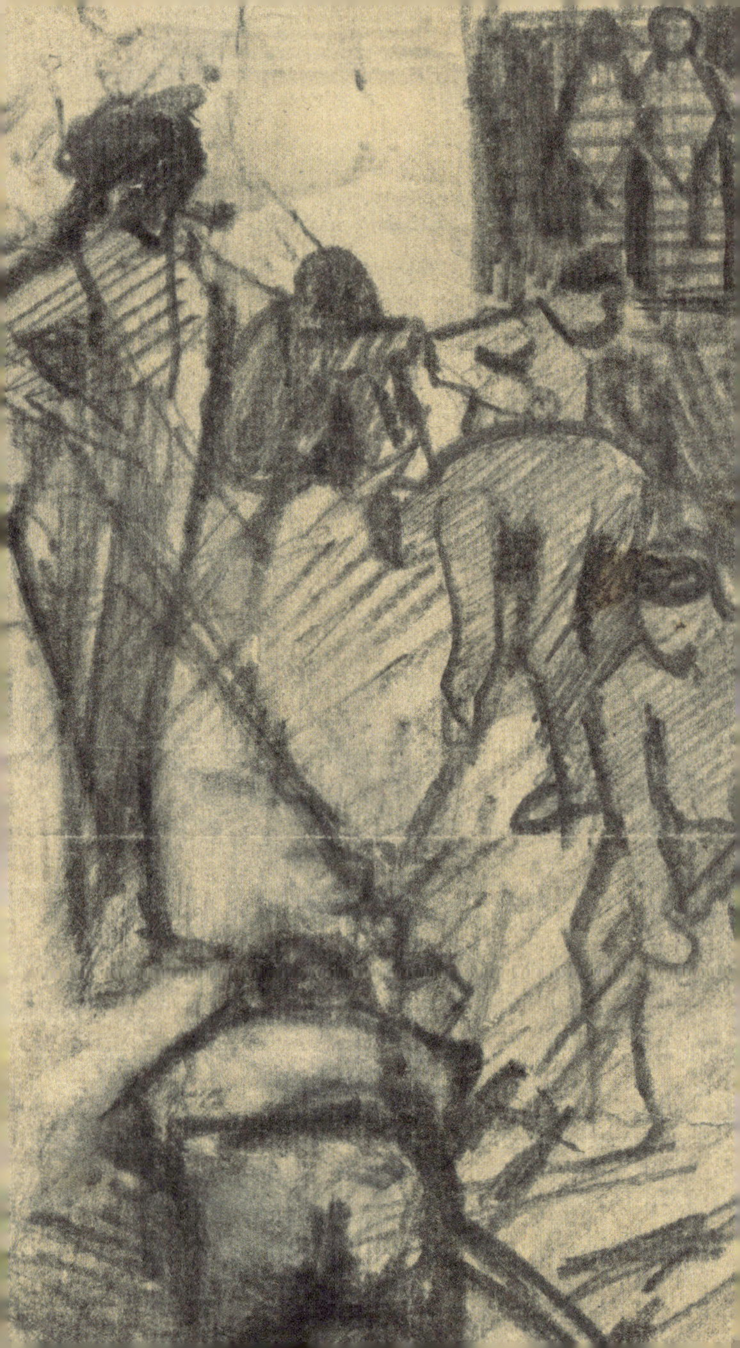

'… one must work and be bold if one really wants to live.'

*To Theo van Gogh*
*Thursday, 9 April 1885*
*Nuenen*



ADVICE FOR
THE SOUL

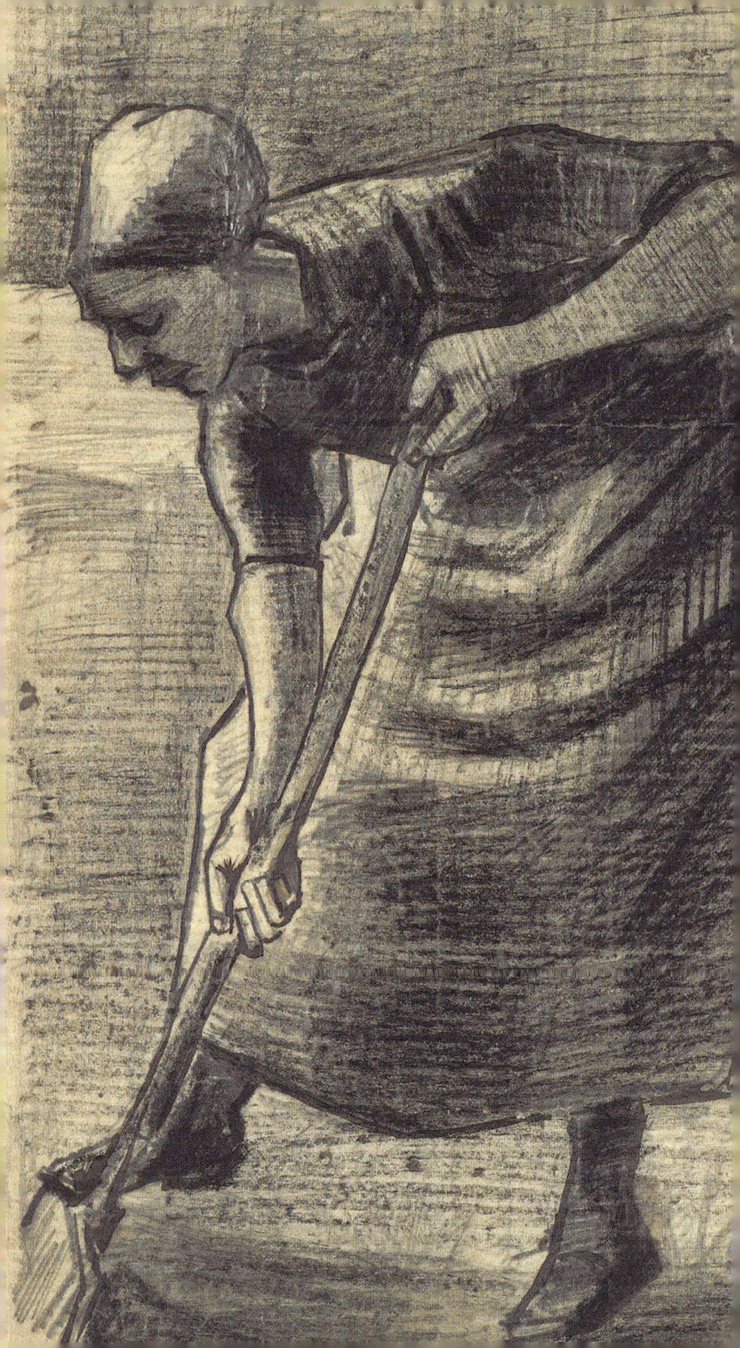

'But if one wants to grow, one must fall into the earth.'

*To Theo van Gogh*
*Sunday, 28 October 1883*
*Nieuw-Amsterdam*

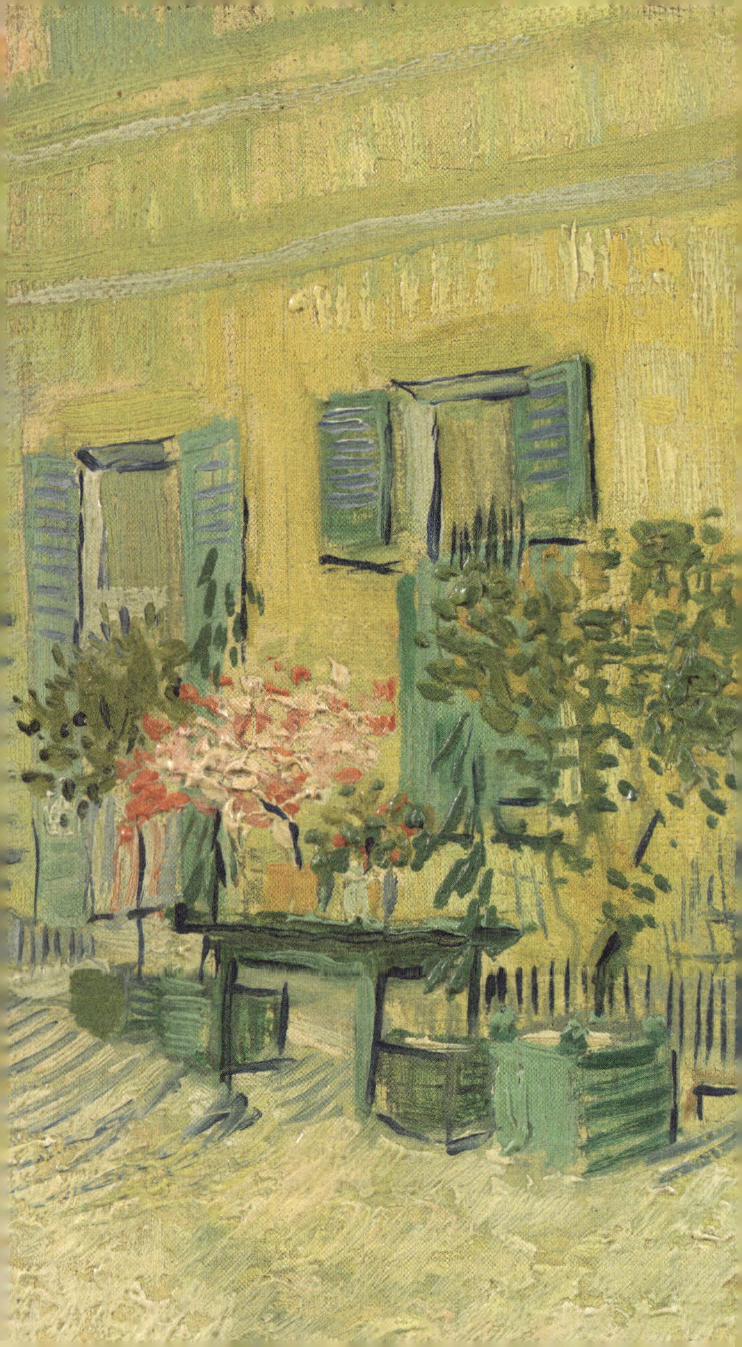

'Have you seen anything beautiful recently?'

*To Theo van Gogh*
*between Tuesday, 1 and Wednesday,*
*16 April 1879*
*Wasmes*

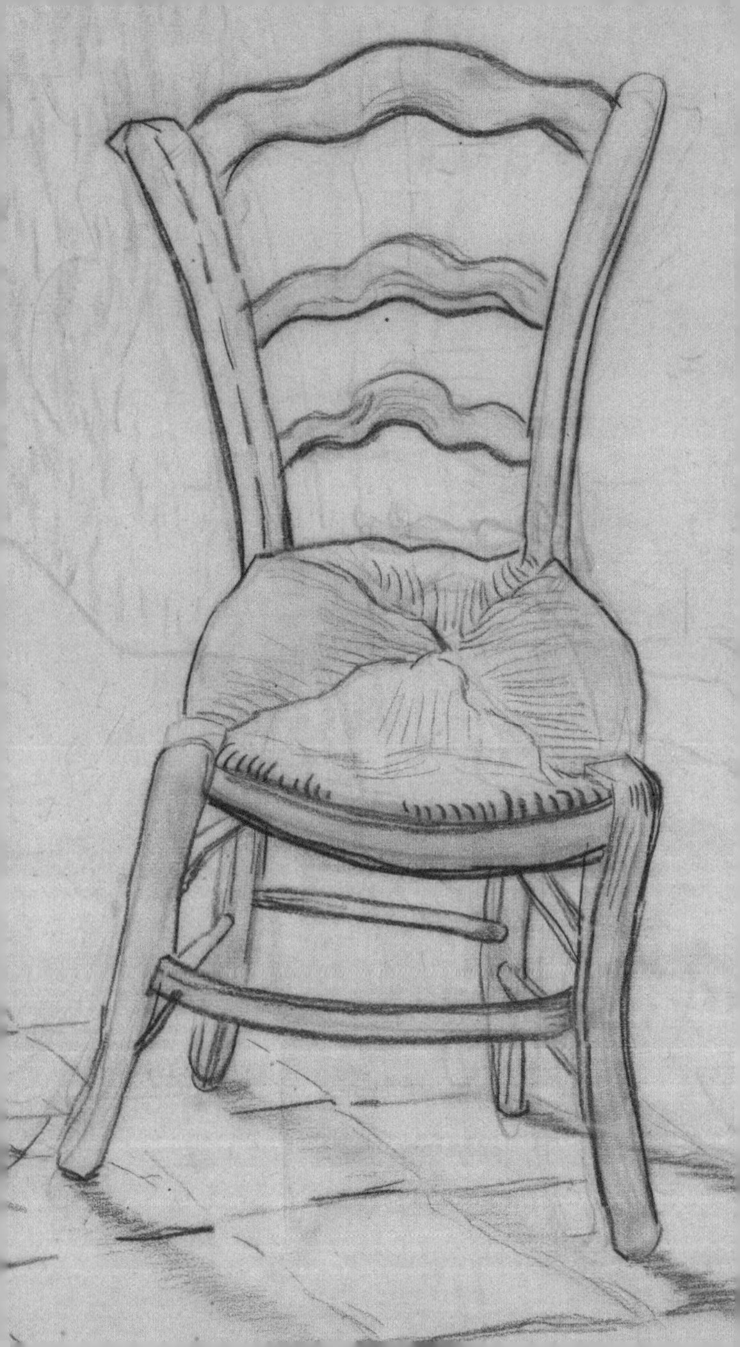

'… I'm in agreement with you that perhaps it's better to attack things with simplicity than to seek abstractions.'

*To Theo van Gogh*
*on or about Tuesday, 19 November 1889*
*Saint-Rémy-de-Provence*

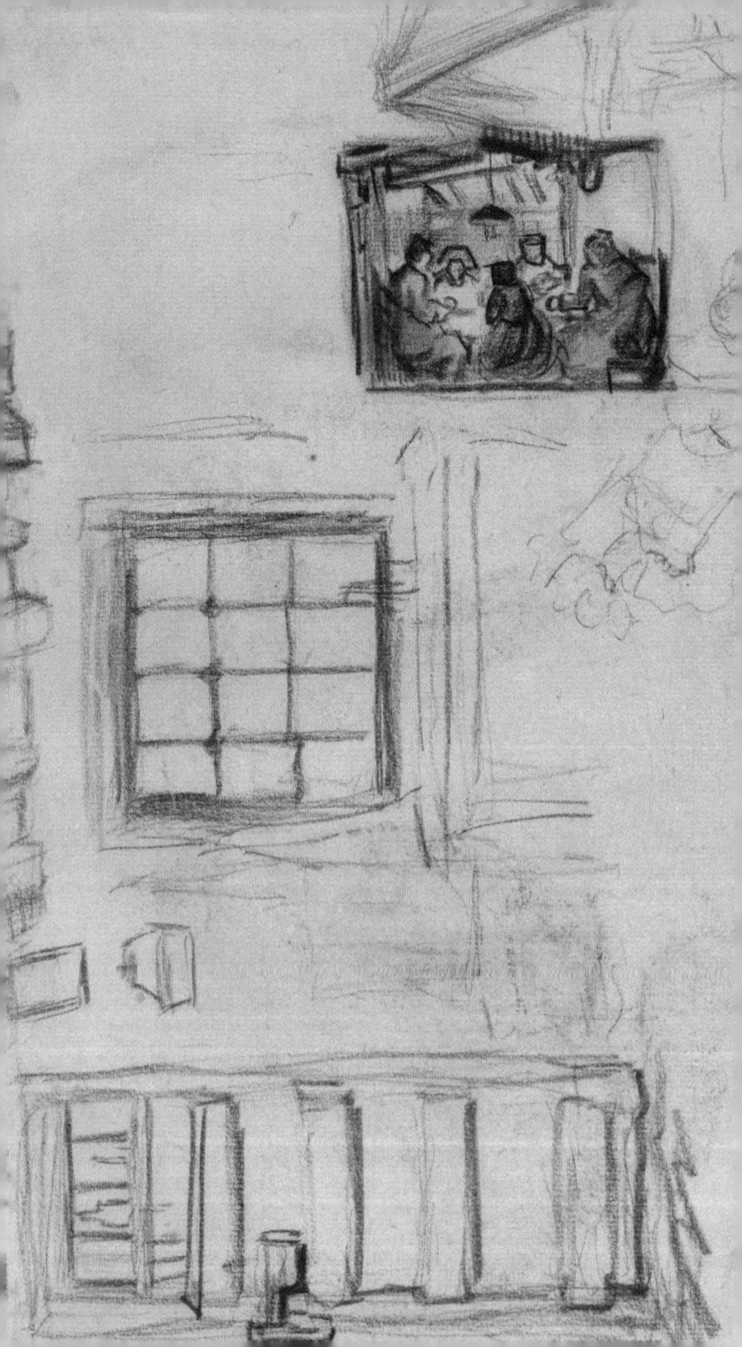

'We are merely links in the chain.'

*To Theo van Gogh*
*Monday, 28 January 1889*
*Arles*

LOVE

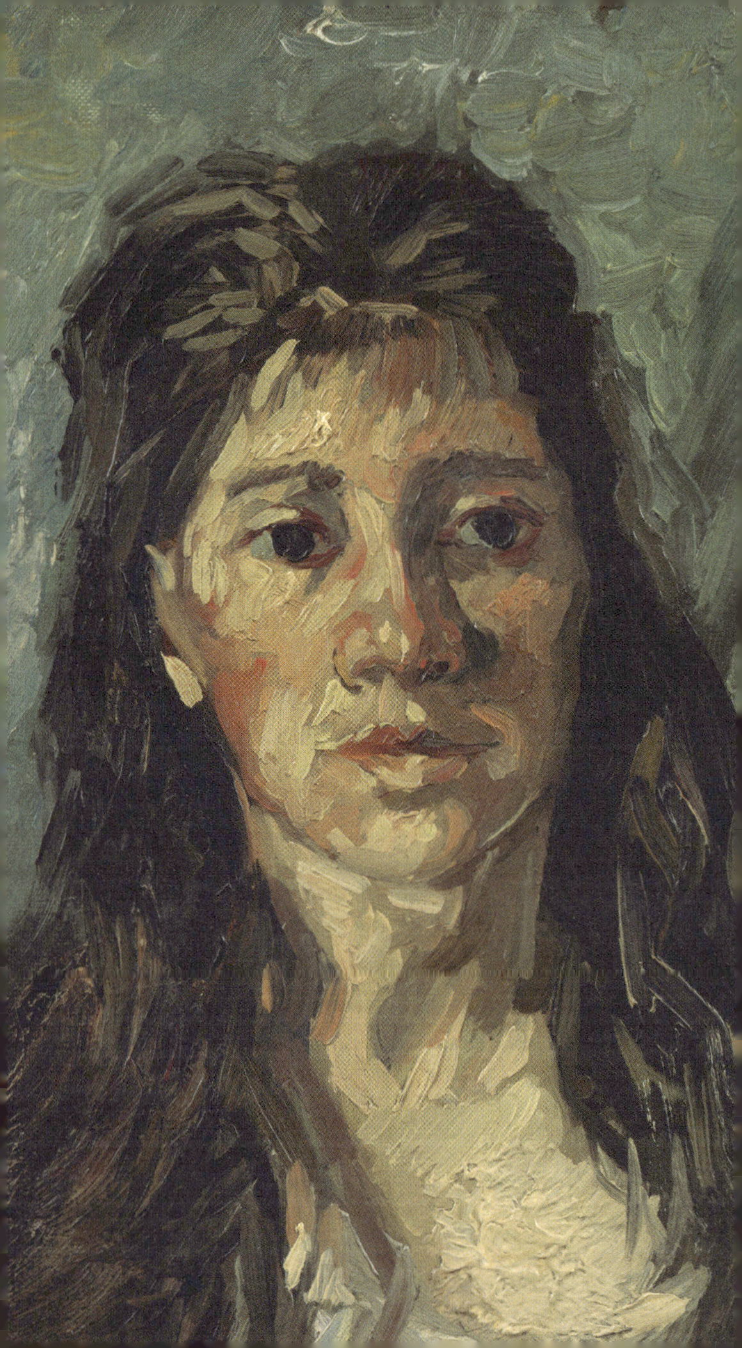

'I've acquired a great appetite for life and I'm very glad that I love. My life and my love are one.'

*To Theo van Gogh*
*Monday, 7 November 1881*
*Etten*

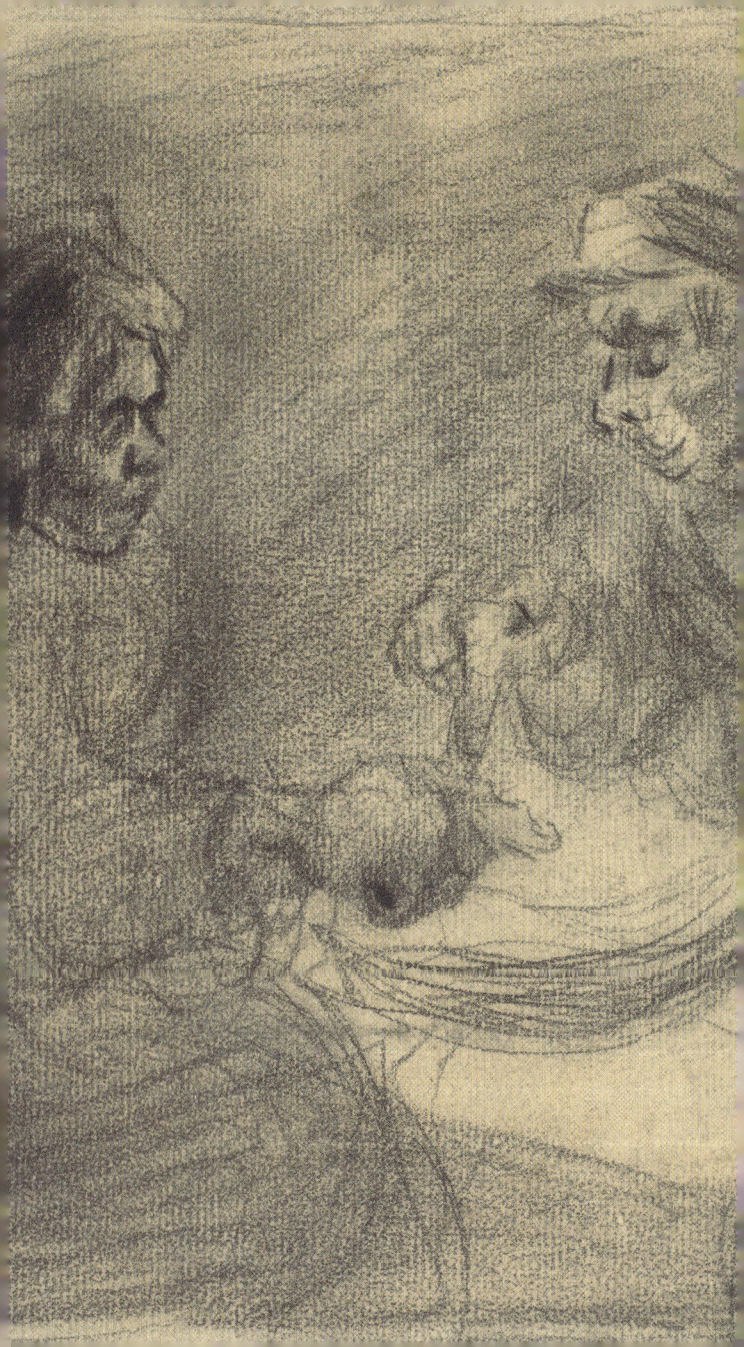

'Love always causes trouble, that's true,
but in its favour, it energizes.'

*To Theo van Gogh*
*between about Wednesday, 5*
*and about Sunday, 9 March 1884*
*Nuenen*

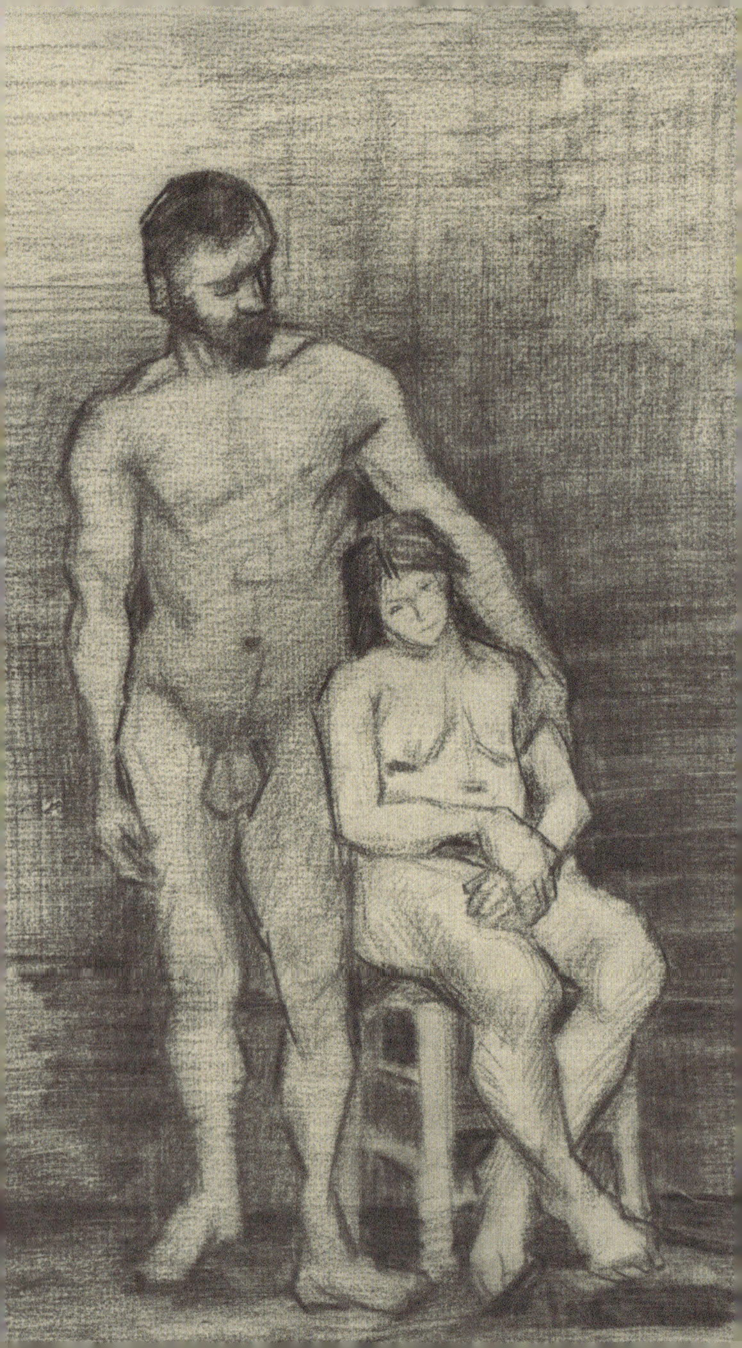

'I'm just a man of human passions, and for as long as I walk "down here" on the heath, I don't have time to worry about a celestial, mystical love, as long as I feel another, of a more frank and earthly nature. I do need the beautiful and the sublime, I admit it, but first of all I also need something other than that – to start with – kindness and good will, tenderness …'

*To Anthon van Rappard*
*Saturday, 12 November 1881*
*Etten*

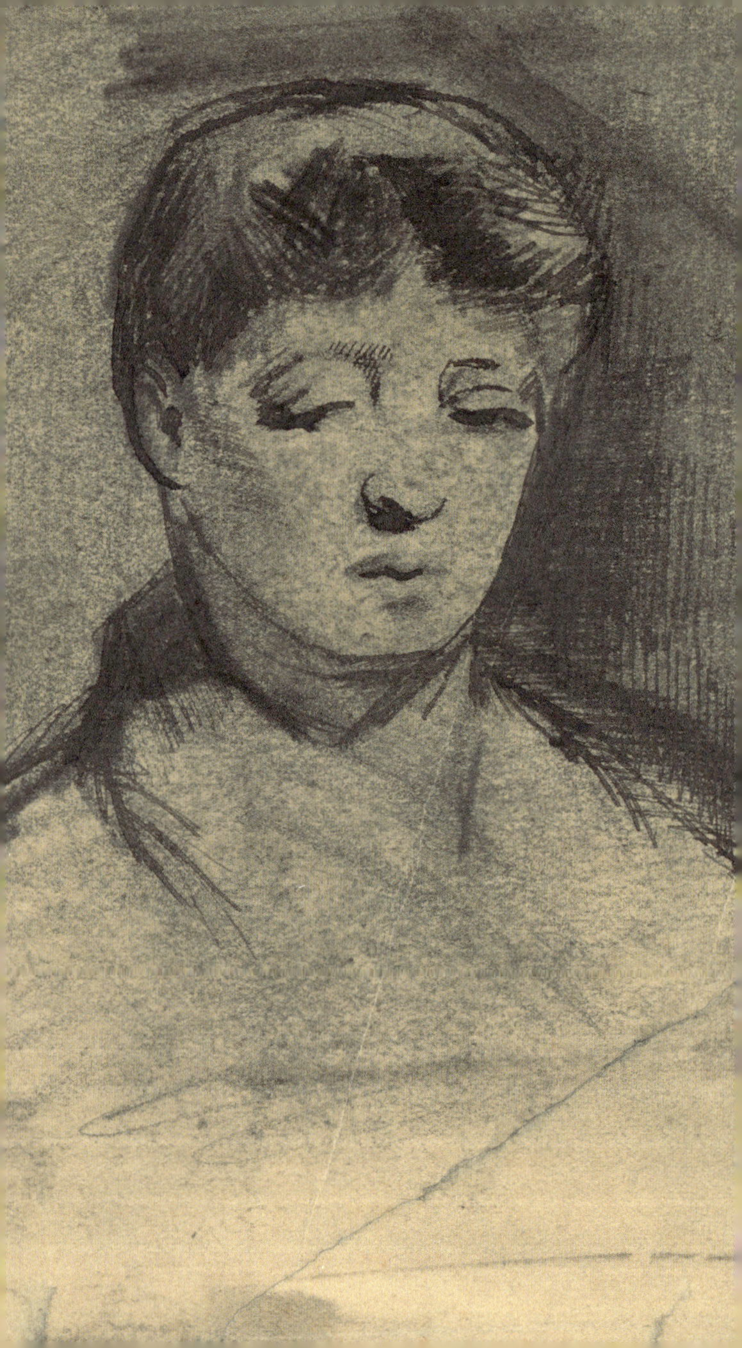

'… but look, I love, and how could I feel love if I myself weren't alive and others weren't alive?'

*To Theo van Gogh*
*on or about Friday, 23 December 1881*
*Etten*

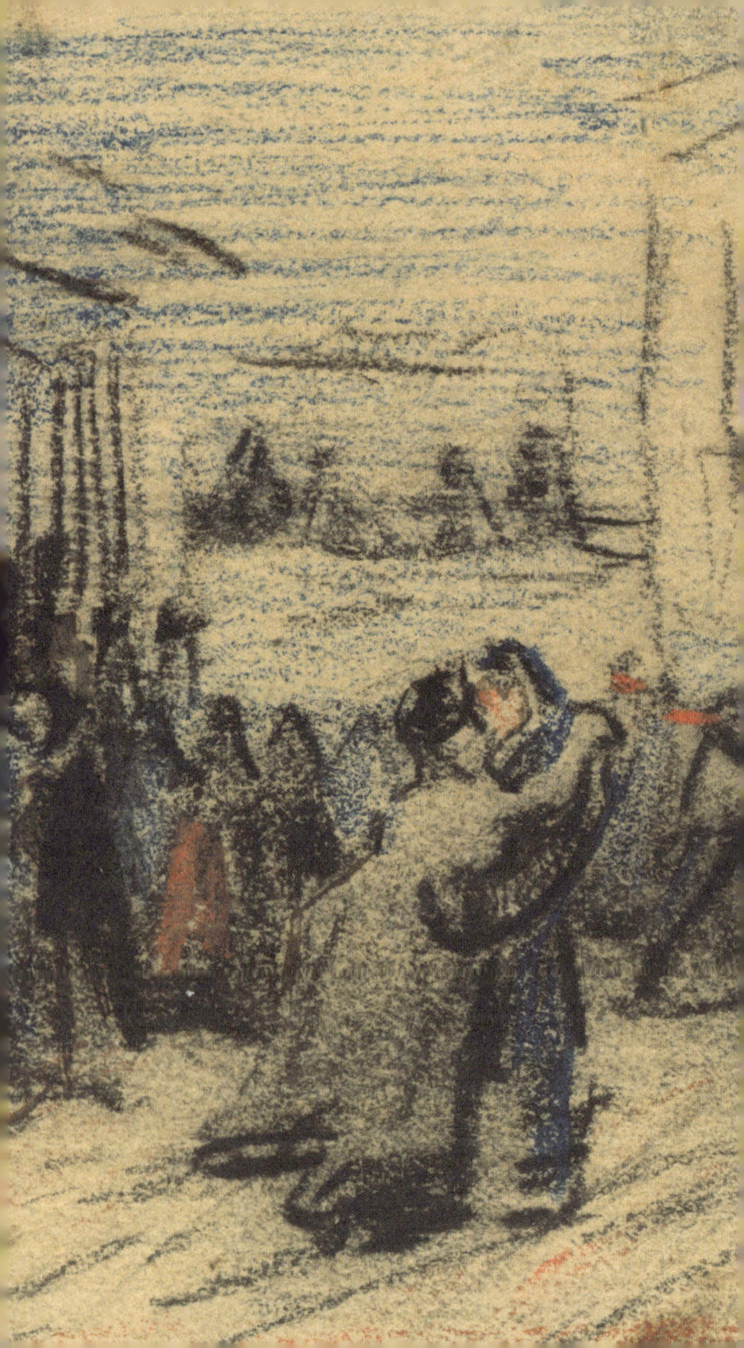

'Love is sometimes blessed, although the
world seems to believe it should doubt this.
But the blessing lies in the fact that one
can do more by working with love than
otherwise, and one fears less.'

*To Theo van Gogh*
*Sunday, 3 June 1883*
*The Hague*

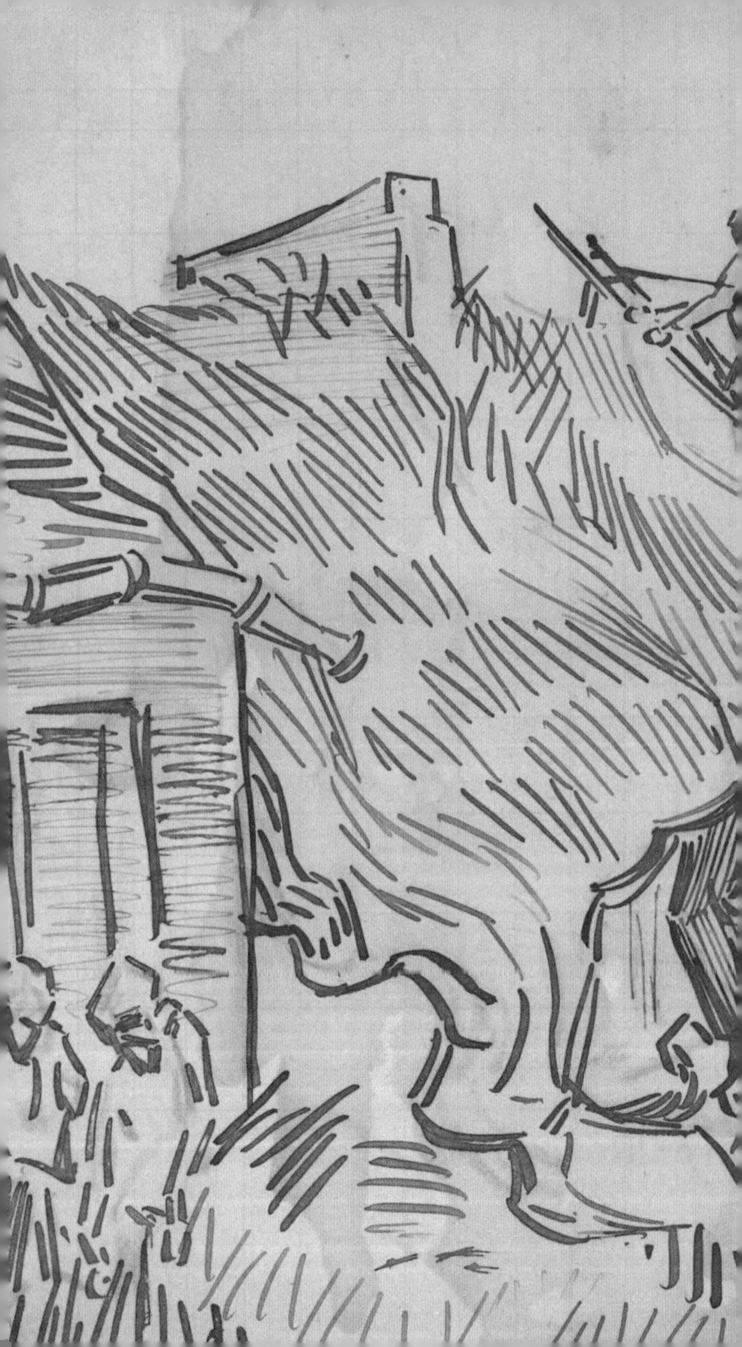

'But without intending it, I'm always
inclined to believe that the best way
of knowing God is to love a great deal.
Love that friend, that person, that thing,
whatever you like, you'll be on the
right path to knowing more thoroughly,
afterwards; that's what I say to myself. But
you must love with a high, serious intimate
sympathy, with a will, with intelligence,
and you must always seek to know more
thoroughly, better, and more. That leads
to God, that leads to unshakeable faith.'

*To Theo van Gogh*
*between about Tuesday, 22*
*and Thursday, 24 June 1880*
*Cuesmes*

SOUL

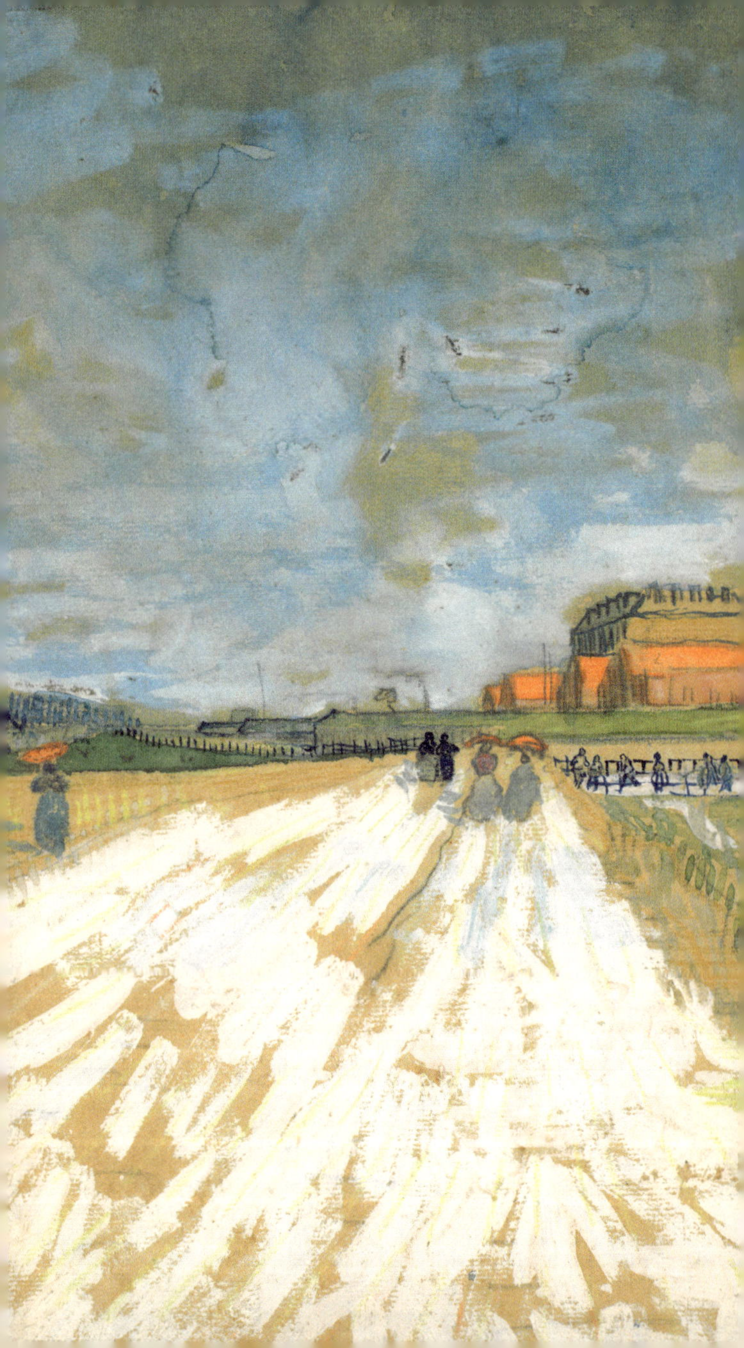

'… because if one has fire in one, and soul, one can't keep stifling them and – one would rather burn than suffocate. What's inside must get out.'

*To Willemien van Gogh*
*late October 1887*
*Paris*



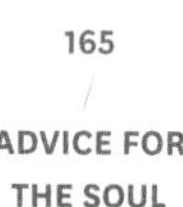

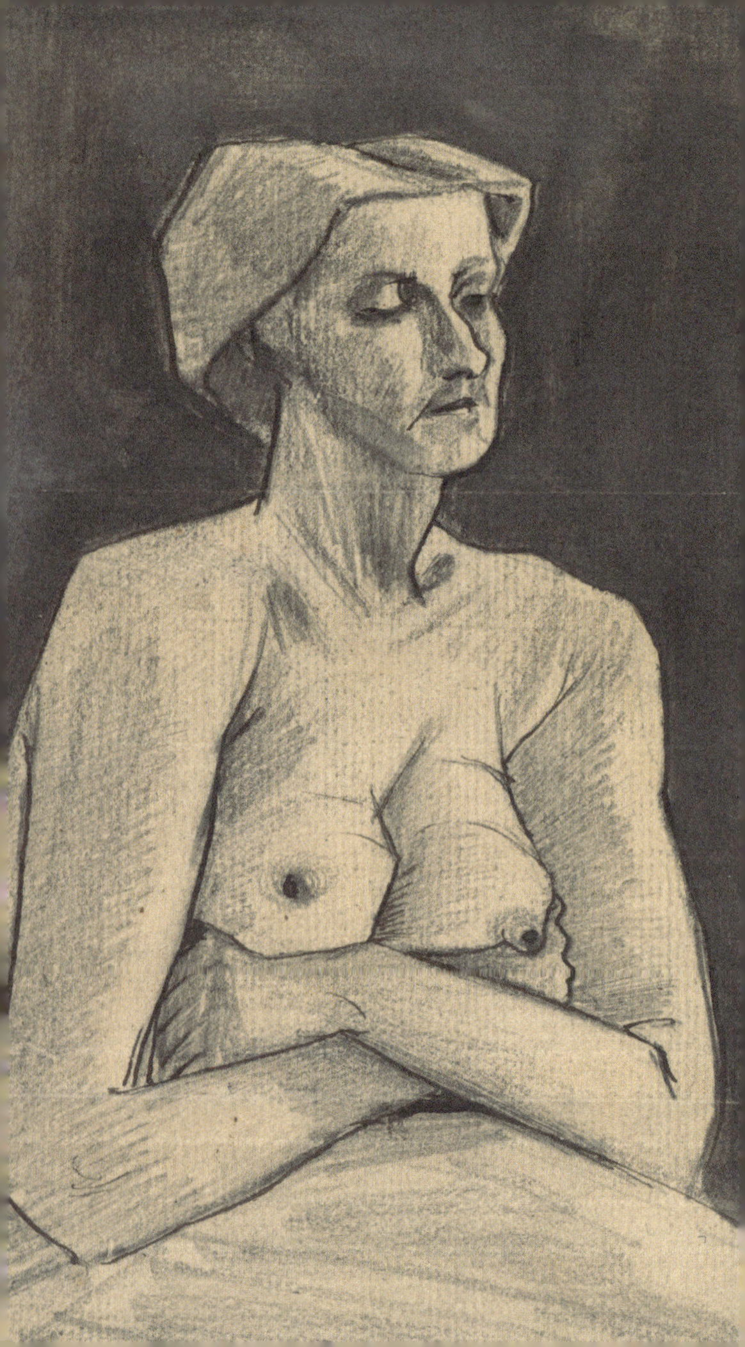

'Purity of soul and impurity of body can go together.'

*To Theo van Gogh*
*Monday, 10 August 1874*
*London*



ADVICE FOR
THE SOUL

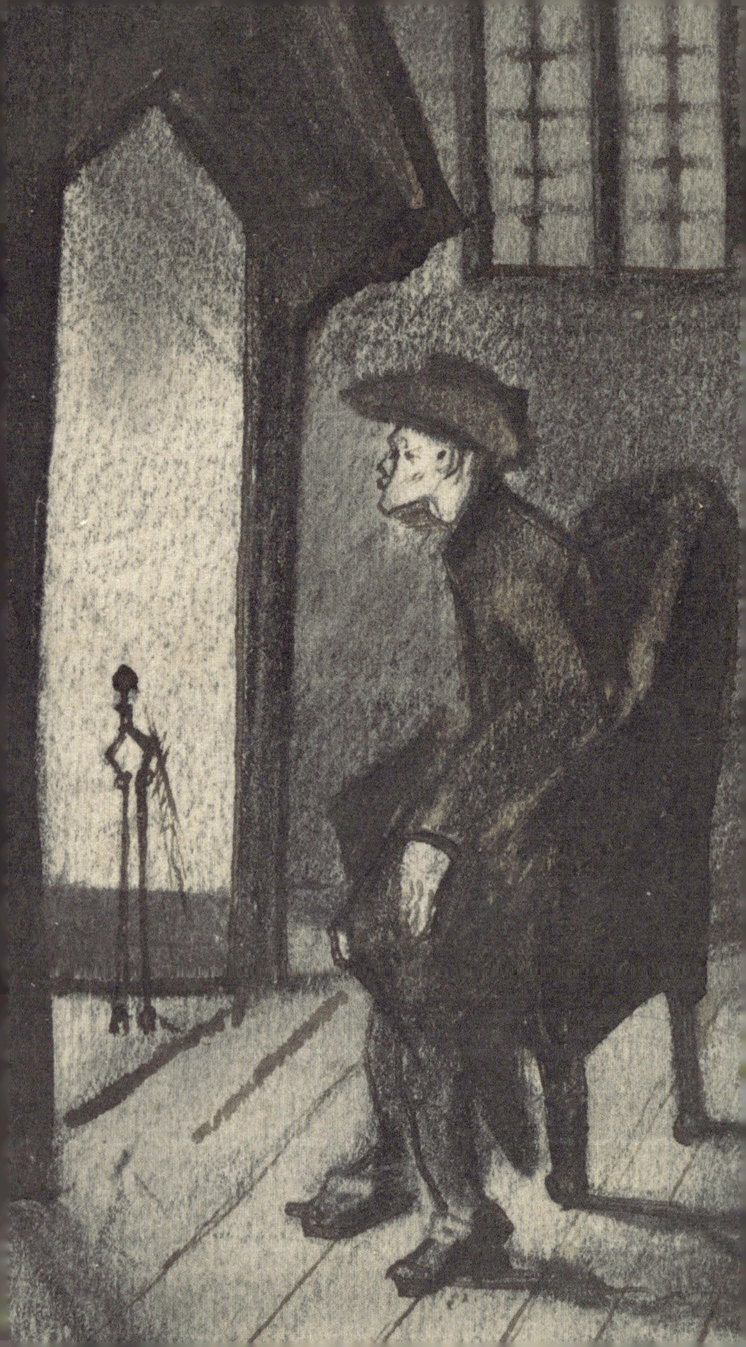

'… it seems to me that one of the strongest
pieces of evidence for the existence
of "something on high" in which Millet
believed, namely in the existence of a God
and an eternity, is the unutterably moving
quality that there can be in the expression
of an old man like that, without his being
aware of it perhaps, as he sits so quietly in
the corner of his hearth. At the same time
something precious, something noble, that
can't be meant for the worms.'

*To Theo van Gogh*
*Sunday, 26 and Monday, 27 November 1882*
*The Hague*

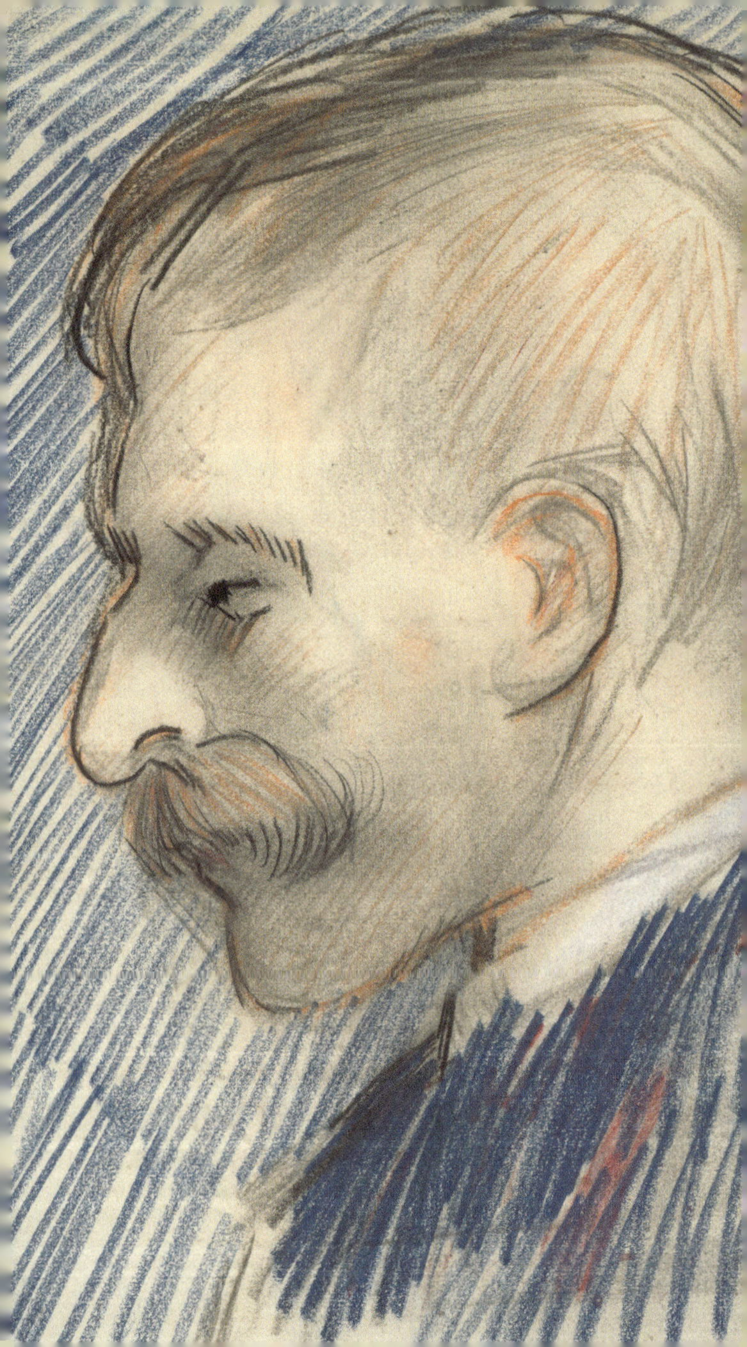

'We know so little about life that we're not really in a position to judge between good and bad, just or unjust, and to say that one is unhappy because one suffers hasn't been proved. … So take it as it is, wait with confidence and possess your soul with a long patience as an old saying has it, and with good will. Let nature take its course.'

*To Theo van Gogh and Jo van Gogh-Bonger*
*Saturday, 6 July 1889*
*Saint-Rémy-de-Provence*

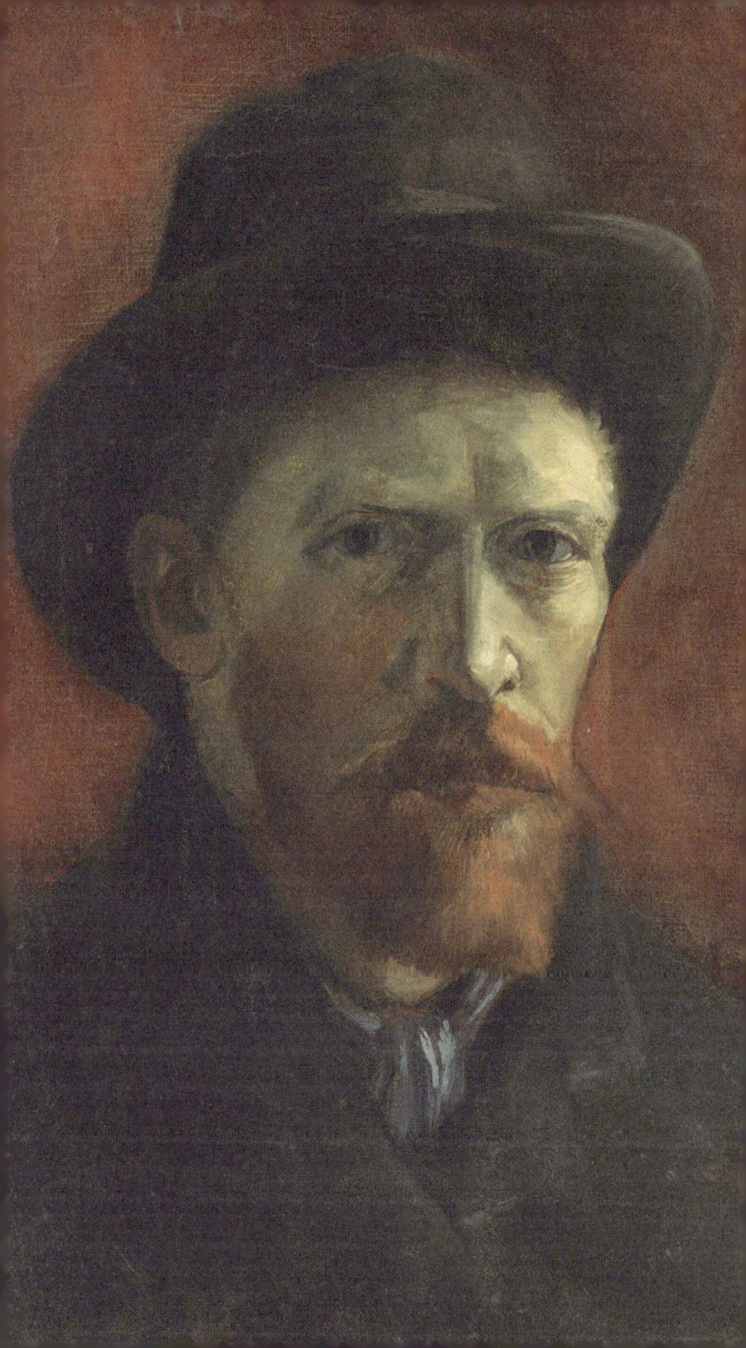

'And painted portraits have a life of their own that comes from deep in the soul of the painter and where the machine can't go.'

*To Theo van Gogh*
*Monday, 14 December 1885*
*Antwerp*

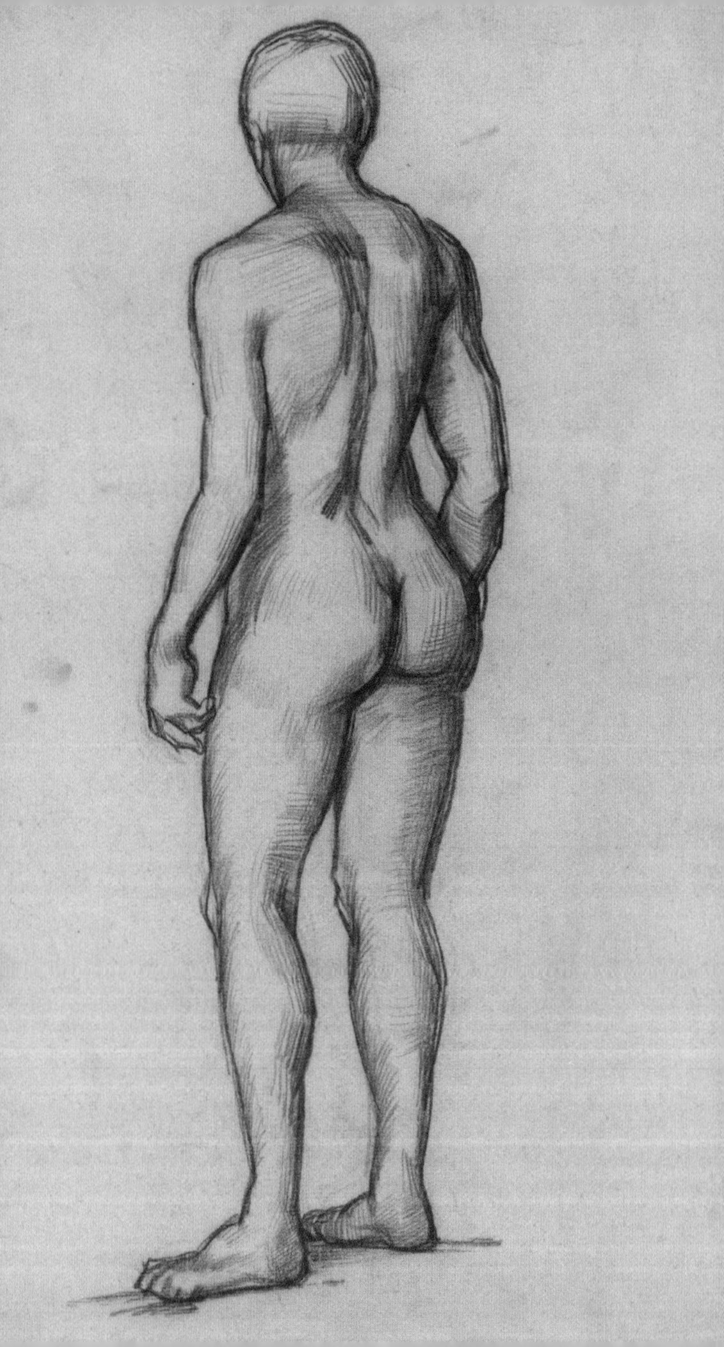

'The question is simply whether one takes the soul or the clothes as one's starting-point ...'

*To Theo van Gogh*
*Monday, 28 December 1885*
*Antwerp*

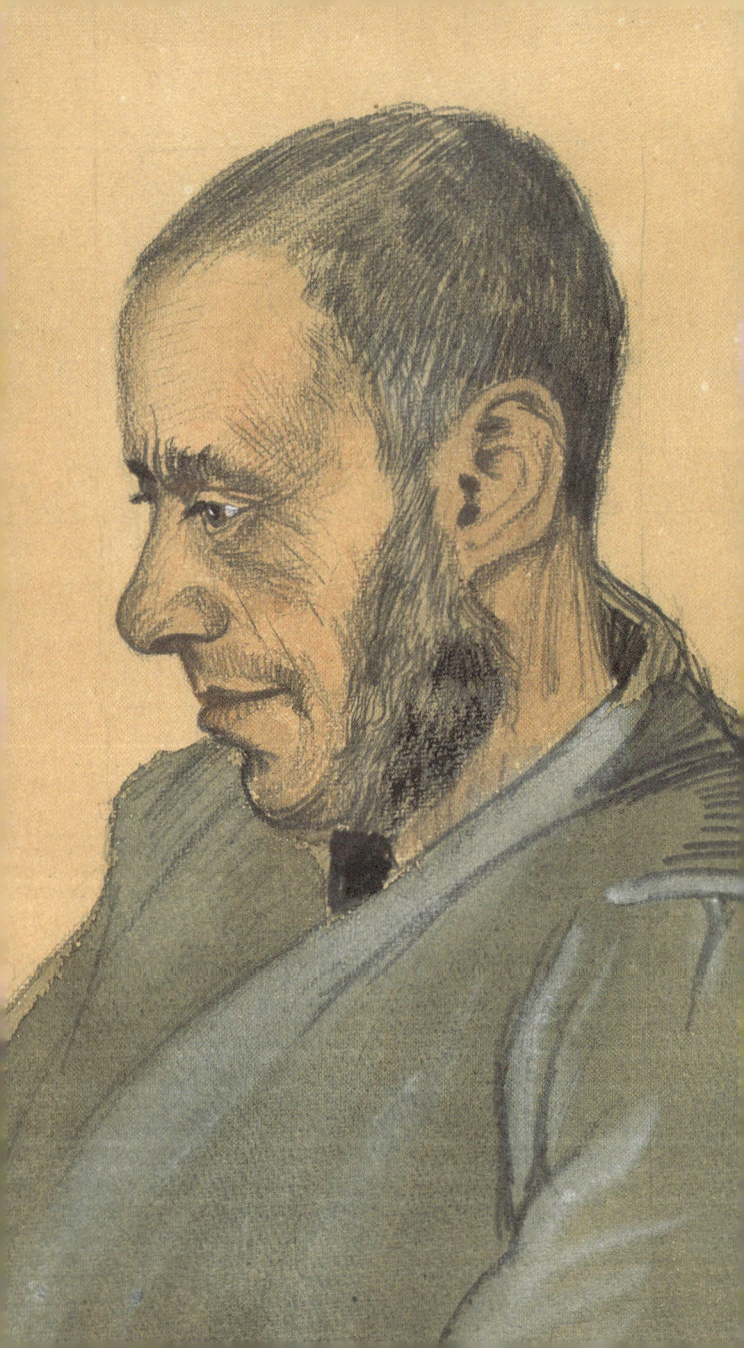

'How much character there is in that face and in those grey eyes … It's good to remember such faces, because it's food for the soul.'

*To Theo van Gogh*
*Sunday, 21 October 1877*
*Amsterdam*

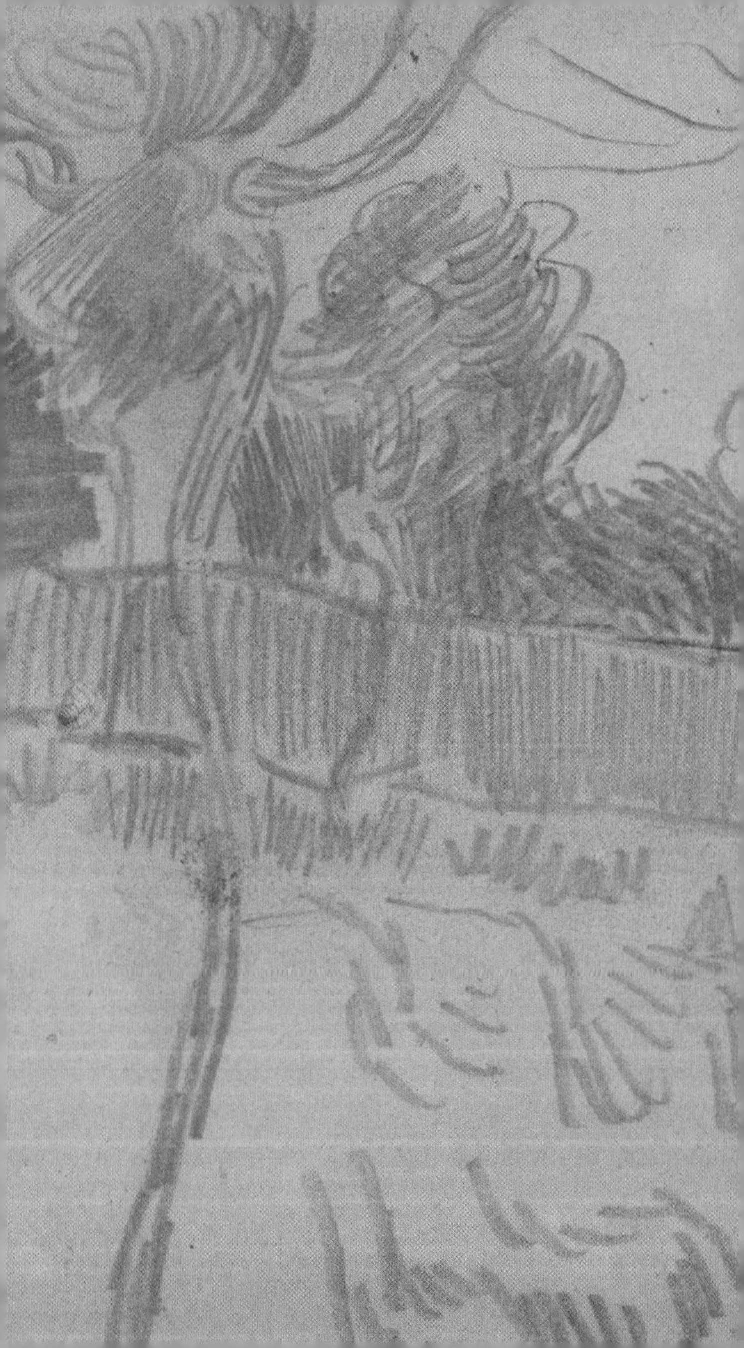

'I don't say, far, very far be it for me to say that I have a white ray, but I'm not embarrassed to say that *it exists*, that *white* light – and I seek it, that alone do I consider simple. …

'And now, I say as brother to brother, as friend to friend, although our youth was austere and went against the grain, *from now on* let's seek the gentle light, since I know no other name for it but the white ray or goodness. Not regarding ourselves as already having acquired it, of course, but searching for it, believing in it with collier's faith.'

*To Theo van Gogh*
*on or about Monday, 5 November 1883*
*Nieuw-Amsterdam*

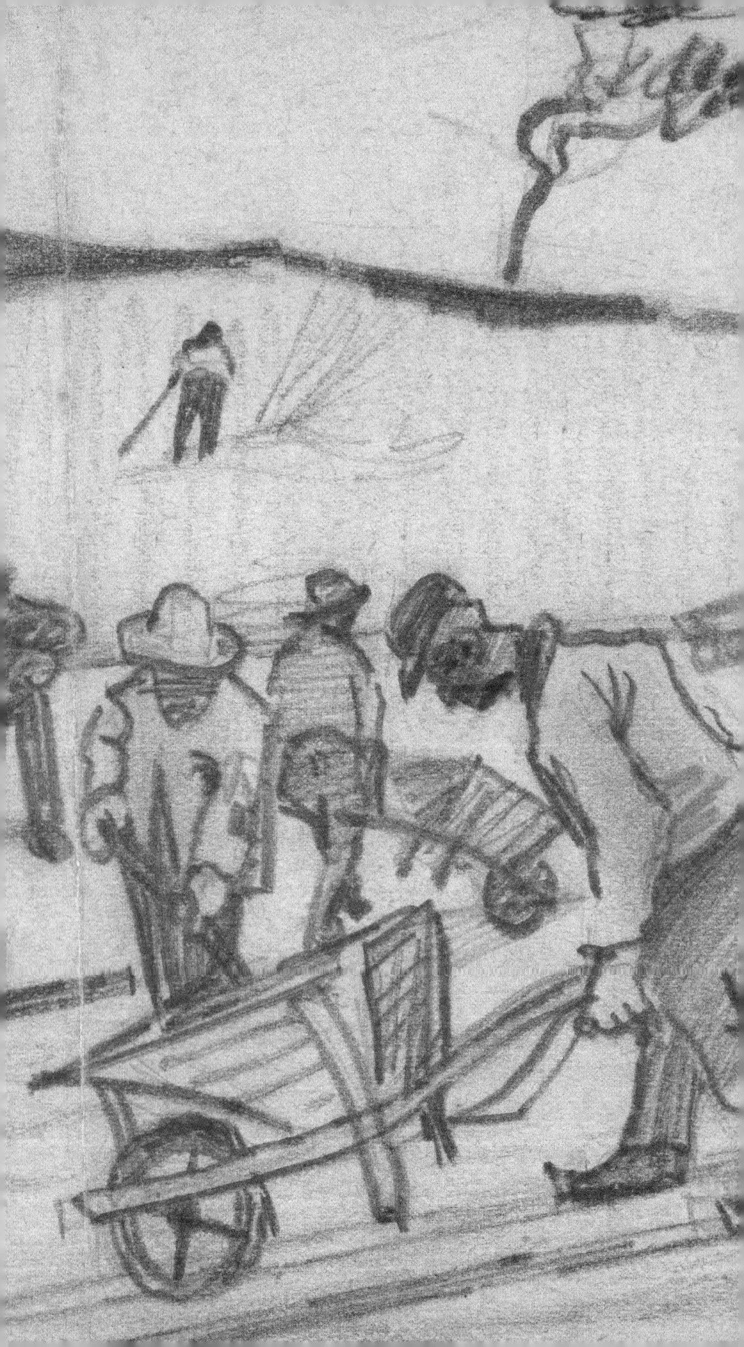

'And if one has to see to it that one learns something by experience, it would be mightily pleasant if one was good and the world was good &c. – yes indeed – but it seems to me that one increasingly comes to realize that we ourselves are as bad as the world in general – of which we are a speck of dust – and the world as bad as we are – whether one does one's very best or acts more indifferently, it always becomes something else – works out differently – from what one actually wanted. But whether it turns out better or worse, happier or unhappier, doing something is better than doing *nothing*.'

*To Theo van Gogh*
*between about Wednesday, 5*
*and about Sunday, 9 March 1884*
*Nuenen*

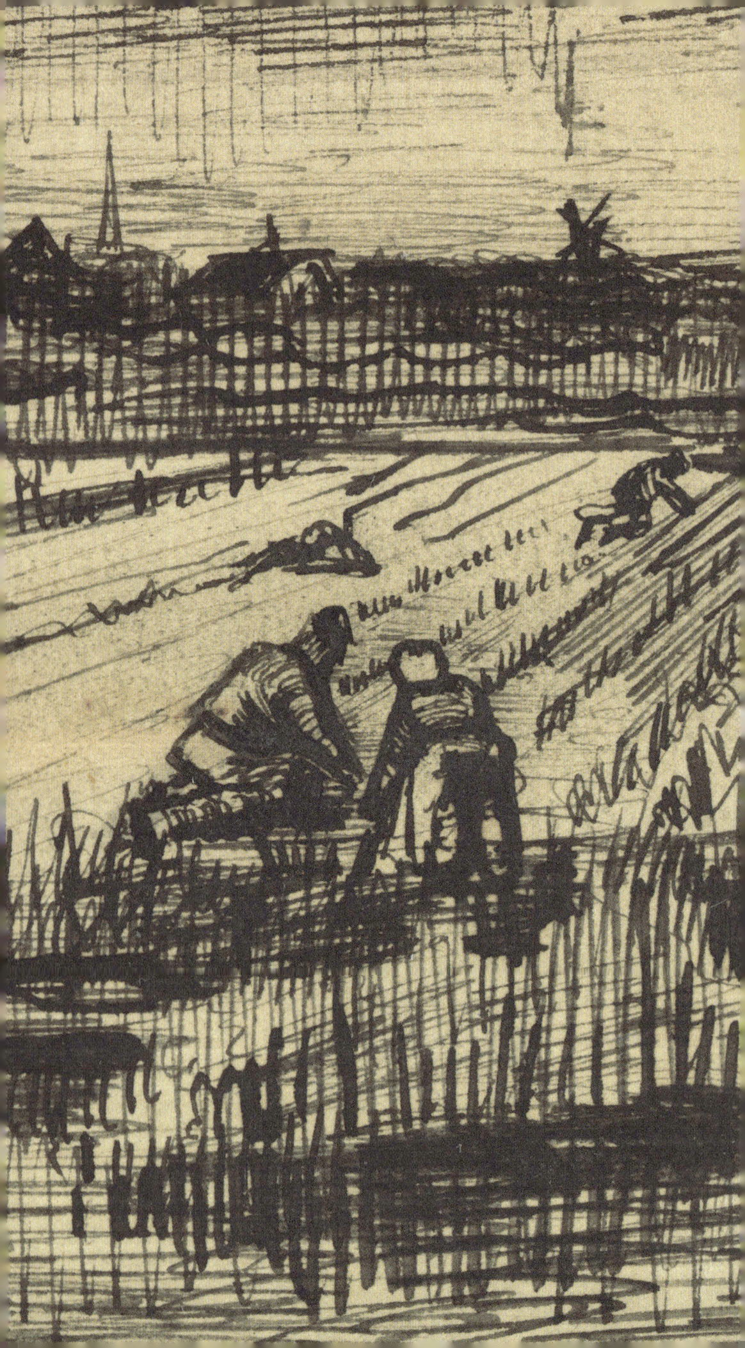

'There's so much of interest in the present
age when one thinks how very possible it
is that we may well yet see the beginning
of the end of a society. And just as there
is infinite poetry in the autumn or in
a sunset, and then there's so much soul
and mysterious endeavour in nature,
so it is now.'

*To Theo van Gogh*
*on or about Saturday, 6 February 1886*
*Antwerp*

amice Rappard,

hier nog eenige der gedichten van Jules Breton
[illegible] je niet hebt wil ik je ze ze by zonder treff-
ellen. Vandaag heb ik een studie geschilderd
[illegible] waer je de teekening van hebt - Ben
[illegible] zoekende naar de kleur van den wintertuin
[illegible] die is reeds een lente tuin - nu - En
gieworden [illegible]

Gegroet -

t.à t. Vincent

Seule

[illegible] aumes de velours, sous une poudre d'or
[illegible] d'un trait de feu, nagent dans l'ombre grise
[illegible] delà les toits noirs que sa lumière frise
[illegible] nclue radieux l'astre de mes[illegible]or -
[illegible] en se gerbe, il tombe épanchant son trésor
[illegible] ze nuit bleu [illegible] une lumière exquise
[illegible] route ou - parmi les senteurs de la brise
[illegible] le et bondit la ronde au tournoyant essor

[illegible] la poussière ardente et les rayons de flammes,
[illegible] usement, les mains aux mains, dansent les femmes.
[illegible] la plus belle ière, assise un peu plus loin

[illegible] e est là - Seule - et mord sa lèvre maladive,
[illegible] telle qu'on verrait dans un champ de sain foi
[illegible] crisper et languir la pâle sensitive

'I don't think much of deathbed
reconciliations, I'd rather see them
*during life.*'

*To Theo van Gogh*
*On or about Sunday, 16 December 1883*
*Nuenen*

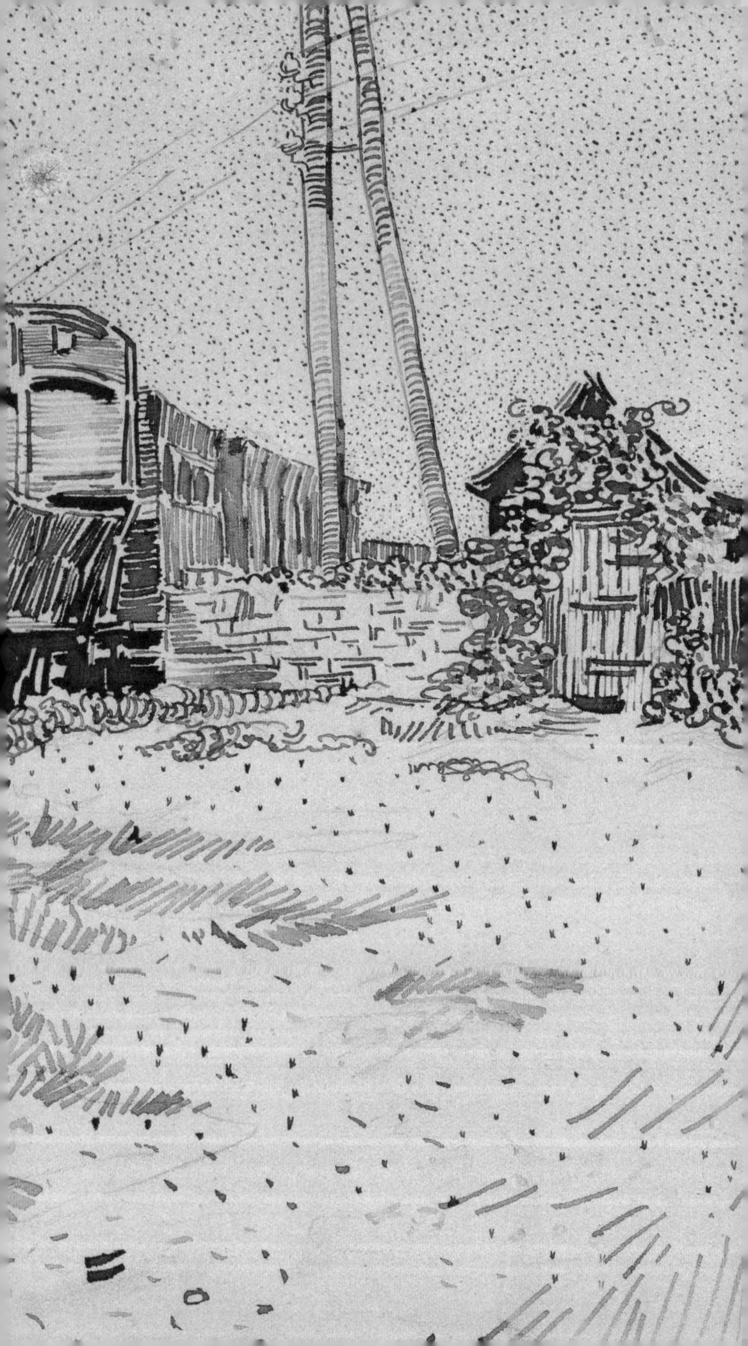

'Just as we take the train to go to Tarascon or Rouen, we take death to go to a star.'

*To Theo van Gogh*
*Monday, 9 or Tuesday, 10 July 1888*
*Arles*

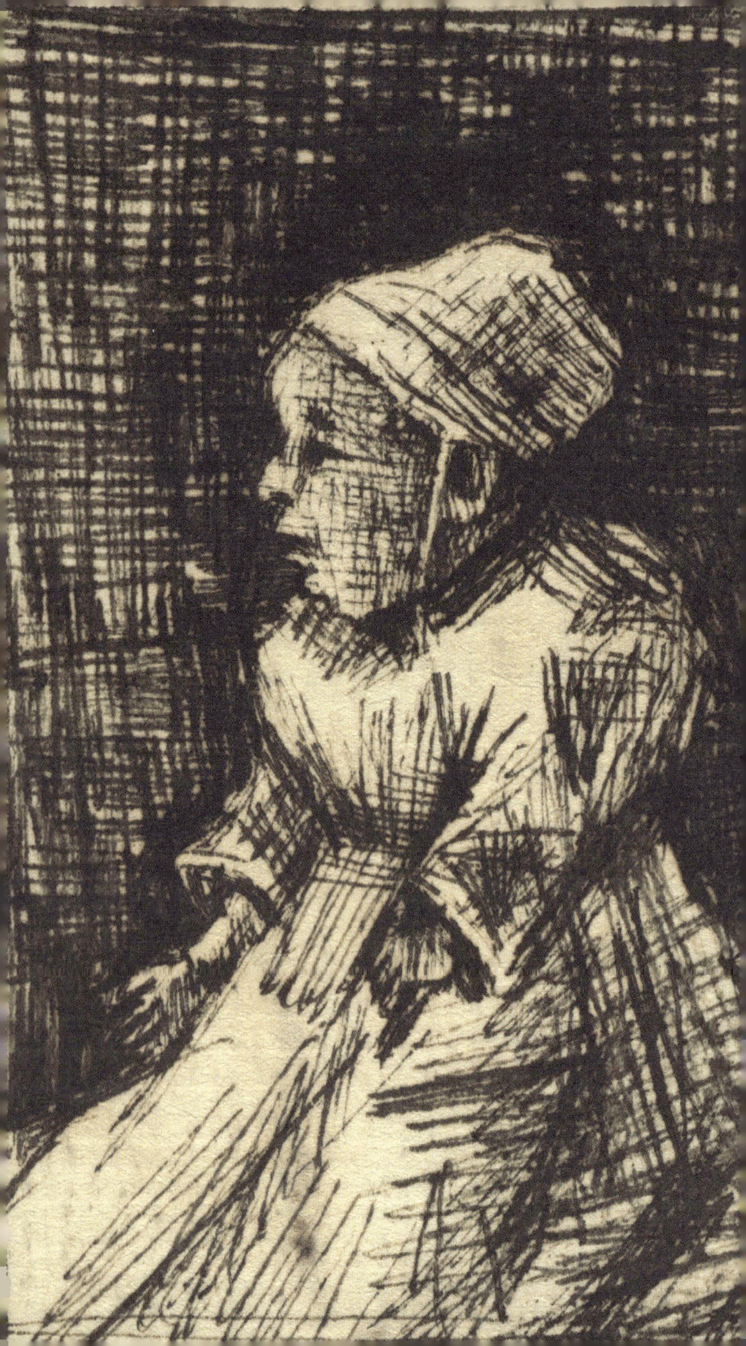

'And a baby in its cradle, also, if you look at it at your ease, has the infinite in its eyes.'

*To Theo van Gogh*
*Monday, 6 August 1888*
*Arles*

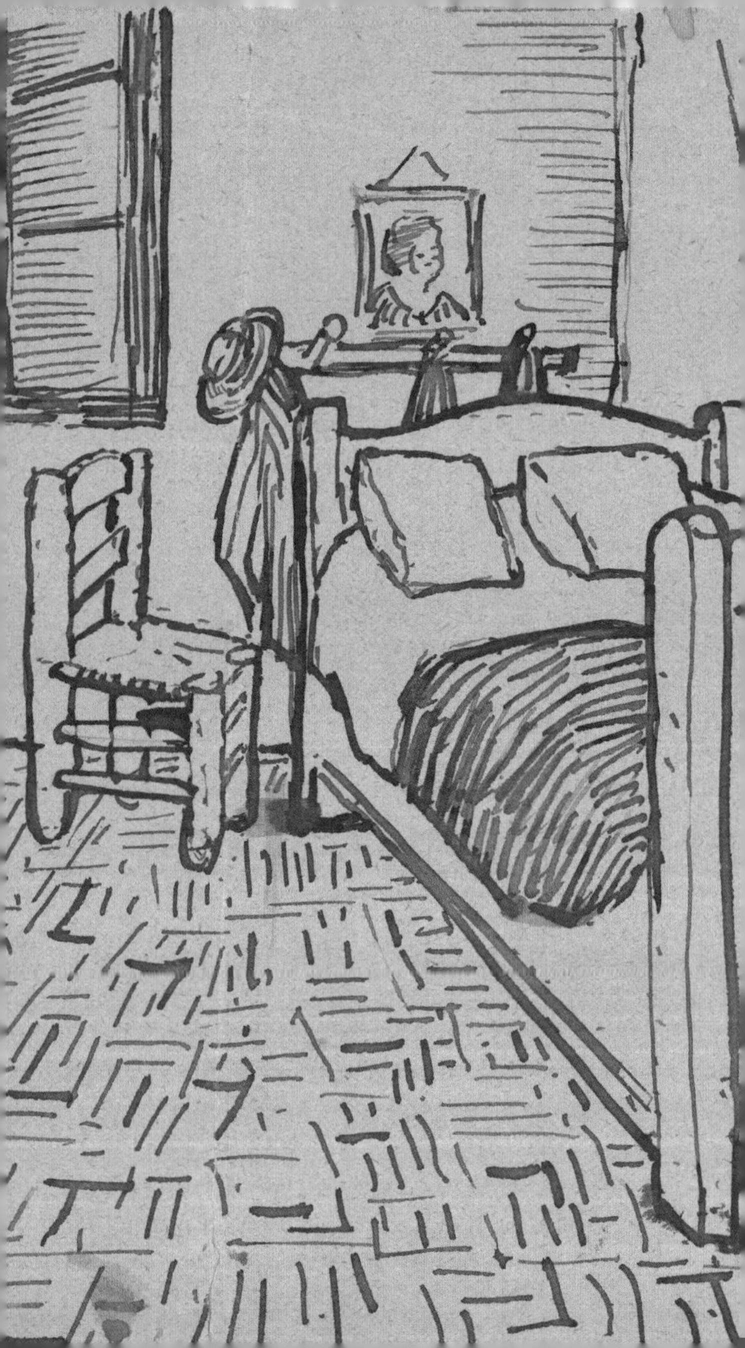

'… until eternity there's a chance …'

*To Theo van Gogh*
*on or about Friday, 7 December 1883*
*Nuenen*